PEACHY

A HARVEST OF FRUITY GOODNESS

PEACHY

A HARVEST OF FRUITY GOODNESS

LORI NAWYN

FAMILIUS

Published by Familius LLC, www.familius.com

Familius books are available at special discounts for bulk purchases for sales promotions, family, or corporate use. Special editions, including personalized covers, excerpts of existing books, or books with corporate logos, can be created in large quantities for special needs. For more information, contact Premium Sales at 559-876-2170 or email specialmarkets@familius.com

Library of Congress Catalog-in-Publication Data

2013947050

pISBN 978-1-939629-91-3
eISBN 978-1-939629-01-2

Printed in the United States of America

Edited by Brooke Jorden
Cover design by David Miles
Book design by David Miles

10 9 8 7 6 5 4 3 2

First Edition

To the many neighbors, friends, and family members who cheered me on.

ACKNOWLEDGMENTS

Many people look to Georgia, the Peach State, as the heart and soul of peach country, but Northern Utah boasts an impressive range of peach varieties that rival their southern cousins. Settled in the mid-eighteen hundreds by hardy Mormon pioneers, Brigham City became one of the top peach-producing communities on the Wasatch Front. Local lore says that, in 1855, English emigrant William Wrighton purchased one hundred peach stones for a dollar in Salt Lake City. He speculated that Brigham City's climate and fertile soil would be conducive to growing fruit—and he was right. Peach production was especially successful. In the years just after the turn of the century, hundreds of railcar-loads of peaches were shipped out from family farms to many areas of the country. An event to celebrate the harvest began in 1904. Believed to be the longest-running peach harvest celebration in America, Brigham City's Peach Days annually draws crowds in the tens of thousands.

As a native of the area, I grew up loving peaches. *Peachy: A Harvest of Fruity Goodness* is a collection of my own recipes, local favorites, a couple of recipes courtesy of California, Texas, and South Carolina fruit growers, and a nod to Georgia peaches with a few contributions from Georgia's oldest continuously operating peach packing facility, Dickey Farms. Many thanks to Ginny Hair, manager of domestic promotions for The California Cling Peach Board; Dan Rohrer from Texas' Hill Country Fruit Council; Stephen Hudson of the South Carolina Department of Agriculture; Judy Justice of Dickey Farms; Ann Henderson, Utah State University Extension Service Associate Professor; Utah State University's Box Elder County Extension Service Agent Michael Pace; Blake Slemmer of www.PickYourOwn.org; and Jolene Gibbons of Utah's Honeyville Farms, for their willingness to share information, tips, and recipes. In addition, I want to express my sincere appreciation to Mr. Peach—Dr. Desmond Layne, Endowed Chair and leader of the Tree Fruit Extension Program and Professor of Pomology, Department of Horticulture, at Washington State University's Tree Fruit Research and Extension Center, for his dedication to preserving and promoting all things peach. His knowledge, insights, and passion have helped countless people to appreciate and savor the full wonder and goodness of the fruit. Thanks also to Monica Holdaway, director of Brigham City, Utah's Chamber of Commerce, for her support and encouragement, and to the many good people of the town and its surrounding areas who have shared their love of peaches with me through their insights and recipes. Special thanks to my friend and neighbor Phyllis Valentine. Before she passed away, she taught me that cooking with peaches is as wonderful as eating them right off the tree, and that the possibilities for their use extend far beyond the usual cobbler or pie. My appreciation also goes to my publisher, Christopher Robbins at Familius, for his interest in this project, and to my wonderful editor, Brooke Jorden.

Finally, it is with gratitude that I acknowledge the labors of early fruit farmers—like William Wrighton—across the United States. Thanks to several generations of commitment to excellence, peaches grown in America rank among the very best in the world!

CONTENTS

AUTHOR'S NOTE

Celebration of Harvest, Celebration of Life: The Anatomy of a Harvest Festival

The Junior Peach Queen Pageant. Proud parents snap photos. Giggling five-year-old girls smile and wave. Hair in curls or ribbons and bows, in best-dress they wait, eyes aglow with excitement, for the names to be drawn of the new junior peach royalty. At a pageant for older girls, a bevy of beauties in evening gowns try to win the hearts of judges as they vie for the chance to become the next Peach Queen.

Downtown, in the heart of Brigham City, Utah, SCUBA burgers sizzle on grills. Their meaty aroma, mingled with the tantalizing smells of fresh-baked Dutch oven peach cobbler, peach fritters, and peach pie, entices hungry visitors to wait in long, winding lines as they reminisce about the good old days with family and friends. Over at the carnival, young riders atop brightly colored horses take a turn on the merry-go-round. Daring teens summon courage to ride the Round-Up or the Zipper. All ages delight in the Ferris wheel: a bird's-eye view of crowds milling through dozens of arts and crafts booths and of the carefully arrayed fruit display that adorns the front lawn of the courthouse.

Early Friday evening, rays of late-summer sun paint golden hues on the faces of children who are giddy with anticipation. The junior parade showcases bicycles decorated with crepe-paper streamers. Homemade parade floats beam with community pride. Saturday morning, excitement simmers. Dozens of local firefighters serve an annual Fireman's Breakfast—a hearty repast of pancakes, ham, and eggs. The Peach Days 10k Road Race is winding up. On the last few blocks up Main Street to the historic Christensen Academy of Music and Dancing, runners push to give their best as well-wishers cheer them on. At the Brigham City Chamber of Commerce, sweet peach treats await: peach candy, peach taffy, peach bubblegum, and even peach licorice. On the west side of town, the Bonneville Rod and Custom Car Club Show draws automobile enthusiasts. The softball tournament brings innings of well-practiced pitches, confident hits, and triumphant home runs.

Back on Main Street, beneath a leafy canopy of sycamore trees, the crown jewel of Peach Days is about to unfold. For the length of nearly ten city blocks, the road is closed to traffic. Hours in advance, folding chairs, blankets, twine, and willing family members are used to stake out coveted

A crowd enjoys the Ferris wheel at the 1917 Peach Days in Brigham City, UT. (Photo from the Compton Studio Collection at the Special Collections and Archives Division of the Merrill-Cazier Library, Utah State University.)

spots along the route. The "big parade" boasts floats and bands, drill teams and dancers. Spirited horses bear riders dressed in full western attire. An enthusiastic contingent of Shriners—each sporting a bright red fez with a billowing tassel—motor by in miniature, lawnmower engine-powered cars. The new Junior Peach royalty and the newly crowned Peach Queen and her attendants parade-wave from polished sports cars.

After the parade's conclusion, there'll be time for yet another dish (or two) of peach cobbler. Children will enjoy a few more rides at the carnival. Moms and dads, aunts and uncles, grandparents and cousins, friends both old and new, will savor a few more hours together, basking in a harvest of memories. For a while, life is a little better, smiles a little brighter; Brigham City's Peach Days is small town America at its best.

In similar honor of life, home, and harvest, I welcome you to these pages, to this harvest festival bound in a book, where simple recipes can be enjoyed by even the novice chef and where the peach is king. We'll discover how to select and enjoy the best, most flavorful peaches. Historical facts, helpful information, and recipe tips round out a celebration of the fruit. Come join me!

Sincerely,

Lori Nawyn

TIPS FROM MR. PEACH

Who is Mr. Peach?

In January 2013, members of the South Carolina Peach Council awarded Professor Desmond Layne the title of "Mr. Peach." The honor was accorded based on Layne's "outstanding contributions to the peach industry." He proudly added the title to his existing designation of "Dr. Peach"—an ardent peach enthusiast, Layne is recognized as an international expert on the fruit. The former Clemson University horticulturist is a noted pomologist (tree fruit specialist) and is the current Endowed Chair of the Tree Fruit Extension Program at Washington State University. As a peach video sensation on YouTube (The Clemson Tiger Peach Network), the professor's detailed, passionate descriptions of the fruit could convince anyone to run right out to a local orchard and relish the experience of eating a ripe peach fresh from the tree.

Layne's father was a peach breeder for Canada's national agricultural agency, and his first job—at age fourteen—was picking peaches. Since then, he's earned a PhD in horticulture, produced the most comprehensive book on peaches ever published, lectured across the globe (he was an invited speaker at the VIII International Peach Symposium in Matera, Italy in June 2013), and been featured in national newspapers and radio and television interviews. He notes that his favorite variety of peach—the perfect peach—is North Carolina's Winblo. "It has a perfect creamy, melting texture," he says, "and a fabulous blend of sugar and acidity." And the favorite peach recipe of the world's preeminent peach connoisseur? "My wife's homemade peach pie or a good peach milkshake. The key is having delicious, tree-ripened peaches."

Mr. Peach's Peach-Picking Pointers

To ensure an excellent peach-eating experience, Mr. Peach (Washington State University Professor Desmond Layne) offers tips on how to select the best peaches:

> There are basically three different places where you can buy fresh peaches: your local peach orchard, your local roadside stand or farmers' market, or a grocery chain store near you.
>
> If fresh peaches are grown in your area, some farms will allow you to pick your own. When you approach a tree, you should look for fruit that are well-exposed to the sun. These will typically be found on the periphery of the tree. Here, peaches are generally more mature, larger, have better color, and have a higher sugar content. By contrast, fruit on the lower interior part of the tree are less exposed to the sunlight and, therefore, are less mature, smaller, have poorer color, and have a lower sugar content.
>
> It's possible for some of the fruit on the tree to be overripe . . . technically called "squish." Overripe peaches are undesirable. When you find an attractive-looking peach on the periphery of the tree, what you should do is give it a gentle squeeze. And if it gives a little to your squeeze, then you probably have the peach that you want.
>
> Fruit at the local roadside stand or farmers' market are tree-ripened. The farmer has already put his best peaches in the

basket. The real decision is which cultivar (cultivated variety) to choose. Many farmers will let you actually taste the fruit, and then you can decide which you like the best.

If you don't have access to fresh local peaches, don't despair, you do have one other alternative: the grocery chain store. Tree-ripened fruit is too soft to be shipped long distances, so the first thing you should do when you get to your grocery chain store is find out where the fruit came from. If it's not exactly clear, you should ask someone in the produce department. Generally, the farther away fruit was shipped, the less mature it was at the time it was picked. For example, fruit coming from Chile could have been picked as many as three weeks ago, while fruit coming from California to the East coast could have been picked one to two weeks earlier, while fruit coming from South Carolina to local stores could have been picked three to five days ago.

The last thing you need to keep in mind is that you should not be fooled by a fruit with large size and a deep color. What you should do is pick up a fruit and smell it, and if it gives off a nice aroma and it gives gently to your squeeze, then you should select a small quantity and take them home. If you enjoy them, then you can come back and get more.

To recap, your best eating experience is going to be with tree-ripened peaches that you pick yourself or that were picked within the last twenty-four hours by the commercial grower. If you don't have access to local, tree-ripened peaches, don't despair. When you visit your local grocery chain store, first of all, find out where those peaches came from. The further they came, the less mature they probably were when they were harvested. So try and choose fruit that were picked fairly close to where you live. That way they would have been more mature, and you will have a better eating experience.

Lori's Tips for Cooking with Peaches

1 The many varieties of peaches are typically sold according to the color of their flesh: white, yellow, or red. White and yellow peaches can have a similar flavor, but white peaches are generally sweeter and less acidic; some describe their taste as honey-like or floral. A classic peachy flavor is characteristic of yellow-fleshed peaches. Red-fleshed peaches, which are less common than white or yellow peaches, tend to be more tart. Peaches are categorized as clingstone, freestone, or semi-freestone. In clingstones, the flesh of the peach "clings" to the stone or pit. In freestones, the peach flesh pulls easily away from the stone. Semi-freestones, a hybrid of the clingstone and freestone, are smaller in size, and have a stone that detaches easily when the fruit is fully ripened. Freestones are the most popular peaches for baking, canning, and freezing.

2 The flesh texture of peaches falls into three categories. Melting flesh peaches, which can be either freestone or clingstone, become increasingly soft as they ripen; their flesh melts in your mouth, making them the best for eating fresh. Non-melting peaches, which can be rubbery or chewy, are consistently firm and are most commonly used for commercial canning. The stony, hard type of flesh is very firm and, when fully ripe, is even considered crispy; it never melts and is typical of some varieties of Asian peaches that are white fleshed.

3 When shopping, select peaches that have a peachy fragrance and that give slightly to gentle pressure. A rosy blush is not always a good indicator of ripeness and varies from one variety to another. Look for peaches with velvety skins and creamy yellow or golden undertones. Avoid peaches with blemishes, bruising, or a greenish hue and those that feel very hard. Another indicator of a ripe peach is a well-defined crease. Fresh from the tree, most peaches will be fuzzy; grocery store peaches have usually had their fuzz removed mechanically.

4 Let's convert. Three to four medium peaches weigh about one pound. One pound of peaches equals 2 cups of sliced peaches or about 1 1/2 cups peach puree. A bushel of peaches will yield approximately 18–24 quarts of peaches for canning.

5 Because peaches spoil quickly, it's best to purchase only the quantity that you plan to use within a short time. To help keep ripe peaches fresh, refrigerate them for up to three to five days. However, the longer peaches are refrigerated, the more the juice and flavor will lessen. To bring out the full flavor of the fruit, peaches should be kept at room temperature for 30 minutes prior to consumption.

6 Firm or unripe peaches should not be stored in the refrigerator—the cold will prevent them from ripening and destroy the flavor. Instead, store unripe peaches at room temperature and away from direct sunlight. Ripening can be hastened by placing peaches in a paper bag with an apple or a banana at room temperature. Loosely close the top of the bag to allow breathing room. Peaches are ready to eat when they're barely soft, usually within two or three days. Never store fresh peaches in plastic bags as this will change their flavor and texture.

7 To preserve the integrity of the fruit, wash peaches in cool water only immediately before serving.

8 Peach skins can be removed with a paring knife, but this tends to waste much of the flesh. Another method is blanching. Blanching is a process that involves placing fruits in boiling water for a short period of time, then quickly putting them in cold water to stop the cooking process. To blanch peaches, dip them in boiling water for 30–60 seconds until the skins loosen. Then, quickly plunge the fruit into ice-cold water. When cool enough to handle, the peaches will be easy to peel with a sharp paring knife. Start at the top of the peach and pull the skin downward. Yet another alternative is to microwave the peach at full power for 15 seconds. Allow the fruit to stand for 2 minutes before attempting to remove the skin.

9 To remove pits, use a small knife and start cutting at the stem. Follow the natural indentation or crease, and cut the peach down to the pit around the entire perimeter. Twist the halves apart. Remove the pit with a knife or with your fingers.

10 To prevent browning and help retain the fresh, bright appearance of the fruit, dip fresh-cut peaches into a mixture of 1 cup water and 1 tablespoon lemon juice. You can also sprinkle sliced peaches with orange juice or toss them with thawed orange juice concentrate.

11 For long-term storage, peaches can be frozen, canned, or dried. For more information, consult your local extension office, your local fruit growers association, or the Internet.

APPETIZERS & BEVERAGES

The ancient Chinese first cultivated peaches as early as 1000 BC. To the Chinese, peaches represent longevity and good health. Chinese mythology tells of the Eight Immortals who gathered to eat the ripened fruit of the Peach Tree of Immortality—grown in the garden of the Queen Mother of the West—to ensure they would live forever.

Peachy Summer Lemonade

INGREDIENTS

1 batch Peach Sorbet (see recipe on page 101)

1 can (12 ounces) frozen lemonade concentrate, thawed

Water

1. Pour the sorbet mixture into ice cube trays and freeze.
2. Mix the thawed lemonade concentrate according to the directions on the can.
3. Pour the lemonade into glasses and add a few peach cubes.
4. Garnish with lemon wedges.

Makes approximately 8 servings.

Best-in-the-West Peach Milkshake

INGREDIENTS

6 fresh or canned peaches

5 cups peach ice cream

3/4 cup cream soda

1 teaspoon vanilla

1/2 teaspoon lemon extract

Ground pecans

1. In a blender or food processor, puree the peaches until smooth.
2. Add three cups of ice cream and blend well.
3. Add the remaining ice cream, cream soda, vanilla, and lemon extract. Blend until smooth.
4. Top with pecans and serve immediately.

Peach Blueberry Blast

This is a fun and easy recipe for kids!

1. Pour the sorbet mixture into ice cube trays and freeze.
2. In a blender, combine the yogurt and frozen sorbet cubes. Blend until the mixture is smooth.
3. Add blueberries to taste. Blend again until smooth and creamy.
4. Pour into glasses. Garnish with blueberries and fresh or canned diced peach.

Makes approximately 4 servings.

INGREDIENTS

Peach Sorbet (see recipe on page 101)

2 cups vanilla yogurt

1–2 cups frozen blueberries

1 fresh or canned peach, diced

California and South Carolina are the top peach-producing states in the United States, followed by Georgia and New Jersey. As the dominant producer, California provides half of the nation's fresh market crop and leads in production of processed forms of the fruit. South Carolina and Georgia produce mainly fresh peaches.

Fruity Peach Slushies

INGREDIENTS

1 cup granulated sugar

1/2 cup pineapple or peach juice

1 can (12 ounces) frozen orange juice concentrate, thawed

1 can (15 ounces) diced peaches

1 can (20 ounces) crushed pineapple

1 package (16 ounces) frozen raspberries

1 2-liter bottle Ginger Ale

Maraschino cherries

Fresh peaches

1. In a small saucepan, stir the sugar and the pineapple or peach juice until the sugar is dissolved.
2. Bring the mixture to a boil. Remove the pan from the stove. Cool.
3. In a large, freezer-safe container or 2-quart baking dish, combine the sugar/juice mixture, orange juice, peaches, pineapple, raspberries, and 2 cups of Ginger Ale. Mix well. Cover with a tight fitting lid. Freeze overnight.
4. When ready to serve, remove mixture from the freezer and let it stand at room temperature for 10–15 minutes.
5. Scoop the slush mixture into glasses; fill with remaining Ginger Ale.
6. Garnish with maraschino cherries and thin slices of fresh peach.

Makes approximately 18 servings.

Did you know? August is National Peach Month in the United States.

Holiday Peach Nog

1 In a large punch bowl, combine the eggnog, peach juice, peach puree, and vanilla. Stir well and chill.

2 When chilled and ready to serve, sprinkle with nutmeg.

3 If desired, float scoops of eggnog-flavored ice cream in the punch bowl or put 1 scoop of eggnog-flavored ice cream into each cup of Peach Nog.

Makes approximately 14 servings.

INGREDIENTS

1 quart eggnog

1 quart peach juice

2 cans (29 ounces each) peaches, pureed

1 teaspoon vanilla

Nutmeg

Hot Buttered Peach Juice

This warm and comforting drink is a great alternative to hot chocolate or Christmas wassail.

1 In a medium saucepan, combine the juices, sugar, lemon peel, and water.

2 Bring the mixture to a boil, then reduce the heat and simmer for 3 minutes, stirring occasionally.

3 Pour the hot juice mixture into cups. Top each serving with a teaspoon of butter and add a cinnamon stick.

Makes approximately 6 servings.

INGREDIENTS

3/4 cup peach juice

1/2 cup lemon juice

3/4 cup granulated sugar

1 teaspoon instant lemon peel

4 cups water

6 teaspoons butter

6 cinnamon sticks

Favorite Fresh Peach Salsa

This salsa is great on tortilla chips, or try it with eggs, fish, or chicken.

INGREDIENTS

1 cup fresh, ripe peaches, chopped

3/4 cup fresh tomatoes, chopped

1/2 cup sweet red onion, chopped

1 teaspoon fresh garlic, minced

1 green onion, thinly sliced

2 teaspoons fresh cilantro, chopped

1 tablespoon olive oil

2 tablespoons lime juice

1-2 teaspoons granulated sugar

1. Combine peaches, tomatoes, red onion, garlic, green onion, and cilantro. Set aside.
2. In a separate bowl, whisk olive oil, lime juice, and sugar until sugar is dissolved.
3. Pour over peach mixture and stir gently to combine. Chill.
4. Store in sealed container in refrigerator.

Early on in my quest for unique peach recipes, I wanted to know how peaches would pair with tomatoes. Spurred by requests from friends who'd tried peach salsas in other areas of the country, I determined to introduce the two fruits to one another in my kitchen. The result was my fresh peach salsa, which has been featured as a favorite in area newspapers and local televised cooking segments.

Sweet Fruit Salsa

1 Combine honey, preserves, and brown sugar and mix well.

2 Toss mixture with fruit, chill, and serve cold.

INGREDIENTS

1/3 cup honey

3 tablespoons peach preserves

1 tablespoon brown sugar

2 green apples, diced

2 cups fresh strawberries, chopped

2 cups fresh peaches, peeled and chopped

1 cup kiwi, peeled and chopped

Did you know? Peach pits contain a poisonous substance called hydrocyanic acid—but who eats the pit, anyway?

Fruit Kabobs

INGREDIENTS

Fresh peaches

Strawberries

Bananas

Kiwis

Raspberries

Wooden skewers

1. Prepare peaches by washing, peeling, and cutting them into bite-sized pieces.
2. Wash strawberries, and either cut them in half or leave them whole.
3. Wash, peel, and slice kiwis and bananas; cut kiwi slices into halves.
4. Wash raspberries.
5. Alternate fruits on skewers.
6. Place on a platter or in a rectangular container and drizzle with Maraschino Orange Sauce (see below).

Maraschino Orange Sauce

8 Maraschino cherries

6 ounces frozen orange juice, thawed

3 tablespoons juice from Maraschino cherries

1/4 cup peach juice

2–3 teaspoons granulated sugar, to taste

1 tablespoon white wine vinegar

1. Puree cherries in a blender or food processor.
2. In a small bowl, combine cherry puree, orange juice, cherry juice, peach juice, sugar, and vinegar. Blend well.
3. Chill until ready to use.

Variation

Also try it with cantaloupe, fresh mangoes, honeydew melon, or fresh, ripe sweet cherries.

Honeyville Peach Mango Jalapeño Jam

Serve over cream cheese with crackers for a party appetizer or over chicken for an amazing barbeque! Courtesy of Chef Stephanie Petersen, www.cheftessbakeresse.com

INGREDIENTS

1 pound mangoes (after peeling and pitting weight)

3 cups Honeyville freeze-dried peaches

3 cups water

4 jalapeños, seeded and minced

3/4 cup lemon juice

7 1/2 cups granulated sugar

1 teaspoon salt

2 pouches liquid pectin

1 Mash mangoes over low heat in a large one-gallon, heavy-bottom pot.

2 Add all remaining ingredients except the pectin. Boil 5 minutes.

3 Add pectin and boil 1 minute more. Put in sterile canning jars (makes eight 1-cup jars). Seal lids.

4 Process in boiling water for 10 minutes at sea level.

Just north of Brigham City is the tiny town of Honeyville. There, family owned and operated Honeyville Food Products, Inc., prides itself on following the actions of its founder, Lowell Sherratt Sr., by treating people with respect, fairness, and integrity. They believe their philosophy of treating others the way they would like to be treated makes all the difference in life and in the wholesome foods they produce.

BREAKFAST

In Hamilton, Ontario, Canada, the Winona Peach Festival draws 150,000 visitors every year. There are concerts, parades, a Grand Peach Ball, a pageant to crown a Peach Queen, and visits from event mascots Peter and Paula Peach.

Peach Fritters

INGREDIENTS

1 egg, beaten

1/2 teaspoon lemon juice

1/2 cup nonfat half-and-half

1 cup Bisquick

Dash or two of nutmeg (optional)

1 1/2 cups fresh or canned peaches, chopped

1 Whisk lemon juice into egg. Whisk in half-and-half.

2 Stir in Bisquick until just moistened, and add optional nutmeg. If necessary, thicken batter with a little more Bisquick or flour. Use care not to over-mix the batter.

3 If using canned peaches, drain well. Fold peaches into batter.

4 With an ice cream scoop, drop batter into hot oil (about 350 degrees) in a deep fryer and fry until golden brown. Usually, fritters will at first sink, then rise near the end of cooking time (approximately 2–3 minutes).

5 Remove from oil with tongs; drain on paper towels.

OR

6 Fry the batter in a large skillet (to which 1/2–1 inch of oil has been added) over medium-high heat; flip once, frying approximately 1 minute per side or until golden brown.

7 Remove fritters from skillet with tongs; drain on paper towels.

8 Serve warm, sprinkled with powdered sugar.

Makes approximately 8 fritters.

Whole Wheat Waffles with Peach Syrup

INGREDIENTS

5 egg yolks

2 cups minus 2 tablespoons milk

1/2 cup oil

1 1/2 teaspoons granulated sugar

3 cups whole wheat flour

3 teaspoons baking powder

1/2 teaspoon salt

5 egg whites, beaten

1. Beat together the egg yolks, milk, oil, and sugar.
2. In a separate bowl, sift flour, baking powder, and salt.
3. Gradually add to egg yolk mixture and stir just until smooth. Don't overstir as batter will become tough.
4. Fold in egg whites and stir until just blended. Again, don't overstir.
5. Pour batter by cups into well-greased waffle iron and cook according to waffle iron manufacturer's instructions.

Peach Syrup

1 1/2 cups granulated sugar

1/2 cup water

3 cups fresh or canned peaches, pureed

1 tablespoon lemon juice

1. Combine sugar and water in a medium saucepan.
2. Stirring constantly, bring to boil over medium heat. Boil 1 minute.
3. Add peach puree, return to low boil, and boil for 5 minutes. Remove from heat.
4. Stir in lemon juice.
5. Pour over warm waffles. Store any remaining syrup in the refrigerator in a tightly sealed container.

Fruity Hash Browns

INGREDIENTS

1 fresh, ripe peach, finely chopped (remove skin)

1/2 red apple, grated with skin on

3 medium par-cooked red potatoes, grated with skins on

2 tablespoons fresh chives, chopped

1 tablespoon butter, melted

Salt and pepper to taste

1 tablespoon olive oil

1. In a large bowl, combine peach, apple, potatoes, chives, and butter.

2. Add olive oil to a medium skillet and heat over medium-low to medium heat.

3. Add potato mixture and fry to a golden brown.

Oatmeal Mix

1. Combine all ingredients and mix well.
2. Store in a tightly covered container in a cool, dry place.
3. When ready to eat, bring 1 cup water to boil, and stir in 1 cup mix.
4. Simmer over medium heat for 2–3 minutes.

Tip: Dried peaches are usually available at health food stores. If you can't find them minced, pulse them in your food processor.

INGREDIENTS

7 cups quick oats

1/2 cup firmly packed brown sugar

1 tablespoon cinnamon

1 1/2 teaspoons nutmeg

1 cup slivered almonds

1 cup dried peaches, minced

Breakfast Cobbler

INGREDIENTS

1 cup pancake mix (a just-add-water variety, like Aunt Jemima Complete)

1 cup peach juice

1 can (15 ounces) sliced peaches, well drained

1 package (8 ounces) precooked sausage links, halved and drained on paper towels

Peach Syrup (see recipe on page 25)

1. Preheat oven to 350 degrees.
2. Stir together pancake mix and peach juice.
3. Pour into well-greased 8 x 8-inch glass baking dish.
4. Arrange peaches and sausage links on top of batter.
5. Bake 30 minutes.
6. Top with peach syrup.

Every year in Peach County, Georgia, a cadre of volunteers bakes the world's largest peach cobbler to perfection. In 2004, commissioners appointed county information systems manager Rich Bennett to head the effort; he first went through a one-year apprenticeship. A highlight of the annual Georgia Peach Festival, this giant cobbler bakes for about five hours in a brick oven in a parking lot. The cobbler—a massive eleven feet by five feet, and eight inches deep—must then cool. The team uses seventy-five gallons of peaches, along with ninety pounds of butter, one-hundred-fifty pounds of both sugar and flour, and thirty-two gallons of milk, to produce the famed culinary behemoth. I wouldn't want to count up the calories for that!

Peach Granola

1 Preheat oven to 300 degrees.

2 Combine dry ingredients in a large bowl.

3 In small saucepan, mix brown sugar, honey, olive oil, and vanilla together and stir over low heat until sugar is dissolved.

4 Pour over dry mixture and mix well.

5 Spread onto two well-greased cookie sheets.

6 Bake until lightly browned, 15–20 minutes. Stir every five minutes during baking.

7 Remove from oven to cool. Continue to stir every few minutes.

8 When cooled, store in an airtight container.

INGREDIENTS

1 cup dried peaches, chopped

4 cups rolled oats

1 cup wheat germ

1 cup sweetened shredded coconut (optional)

1/2 cup sunflower seeds

1/2 cup slivered almonds

1/3 cup flaxseed (optional)

1/2 cup brown sugar

3/4 cup honey

1 cup extra virgin olive oil

1 teaspoon vanilla

Peach Crepes

INGREDIENTS

10 premade crepes

1 package (8 ounces) cream cheese, softened

3/4 cup whipping cream

1 cup peach preserves or peach jam

1/2 cup granulated sugar

2 teaspoons vanilla

1 tablespoon lemon juice

Fresh peaches, sliced

Powdered sugar

1. Preheat oven to 325 degrees.
2. Beat together cream cheese, whipping cream, preserves (or jam), and sugar until smooth and creamy.
3. Add vanilla and lemon juice and beat again until well blended.
4. Spread 4 tablespoons of the cream cheese mixture over the surface of each crepe.
5. Place peach slices down center of crepes and roll up.
6. Place crepes in greased 9 x 13-inch pan and bake 8–10 minutes.
7. Garnish with additional peaches, or peach topping (below), and powdered sugar.

Peach Topping

1/3 cup whipping cream

1/8 cup Lighthouse peach dessert glaze

1. Beat whipping cream and glaze until smooth and thick.

Susan's Hot Peach Breakfast

1. In a single-serve, microwave-safe baking dish, layer banana, brown sugar, and peach slices.
2. Pour juice over all and microwave on high 30 seconds or until bubbly.

INGREDIENTS

Sliced bananas

Brown sugar, to taste

Fresh peach slices

Peach juice

Sausage Peach Scramble

This scramble is a great way to use leftover sausage or peaches!

1. Crumble sausage into a medium, microwave-safe bowl.
2. Stir in eggs, syrup, chopped peach, and cream cheese.
3. Microwave on high. Check every 1–2 minutes, and restir mixture.
4. Cook approximately 8–10 minutes, or until completely cooked through.
5. Spread cream cheese on each bagel and add a scoop of eggs for a delectable breakfast sandwich.

INGREDIENTS

2 cooked sausage patties, or 4 links

6 eggs, beaten

1/4 cup Maple syrup

1 canned peach, chopped

3 tablespoons cream cheese, softened

Cream cheese

4 bagels, sliced

Peach Roll-Ups

INGREDIENTS

1 package (4 ounces) crescent roll dough

3 tablespoons (per each roll-up) peach jam or preserves

Cinnamon

Brown sugar

1. Preheat oven according to crescent roll package directions.
2. Prepare dough according to package directions, topping each triangle with jam or preserves.
3. Sprinkle with cinnamon and roll up.
4. Sprinkle with brown sugar.
5. Bake according to package directions.

Peachy Keen French Toast

Egg breads like cinnamon swirl bread, day-old French bread, potato bread, Texas toast, or thick slices of Challah are best for this dish.

INGREDIENTS

1 small package (3 ounces) vanilla instant pudding

1 cup fresh or canned peaches, finely chopped

1/8 teaspoon nutmeg

1/8 teaspoon cinnamon

5 eggs, beaten

12 slices of bread

1. Prepare pudding according to package directions.
2. Fold in chopped peaches, nutmeg, and cinnamon. Add eggs and mix well.
3. Dip bread slices into mixture.
4. Cook on well-greased skillet over medium heat, turning frequently so toast doesn't scorch.
5. Top with maple syrup, peach syrup, or butter, cinnamon, and powdered sugar. Don't forget the fresh peaches!

Grandma Esther's Peach Cinnamon Rolls

1 Preheat oven to 375 degrees.

2 Dissolve yeast and 1 tablespoon granulated sugar in warm water. Allow to sit a few minutes (to activate and grow) before adding scalded milk.

Tip: Cake yeast is highly perishable; consider the sell-by date as its expiration. Pay attention to the date, and store it in the refrigerator.

3 Add 3 cups flour and stir until smooth.

4 In a separate bowl, cream together shortening and 1/2 cup sugar. Add to flour mixture.

5 Add eggs, then add remainder of flour and salt to make a moderately soft dough.

6 Turn onto floured board and knead lightly.

7 Place in a greased bowl; cover and set aside in a warm place to rise (about 2 hours).

8 When dough has risen, roll out in an oblong shape to 1/4 inch thick.

9 Brush with a generous amount of

INGREDIENTS

1 (2 ounce) yeast cake OR about 6 3/4 teaspoons active dry yeast

1/2 cup + 1 tablespoon granulated sugar

1 cup very warm water

1 cup scalded milk, warm

7 cups flour, sifted

6 tablespoons shortening, softened

3 eggs, beaten until light, room temperature

1/2 teaspoon salt

Melted butter

Brown sugar

Chopped walnuts

Cinnamon

1/2 cup dried peaches

melted butter, and sprinkle to the edges with brown sugar, walnuts, and cinnamon.

10 Place dried peaches in food processor and process until they resemble fine cookie crumbs. Sprinkle peaches over dough to edges.

11 Roll dough up, then cut and lay rolls side by side on a well-greased pan. Don't crowd.

12 Let rise one hour or until light.

13 Bake 25 minutes. While still warm, ice with Peach Honey Frosting (see recipe on page 128).

Tip: For a clean, uniform cut, use unflavored, waxed dental floss. Slide a length of floss under the rolled-up dough one inch from the end. Draw the ends up and cross them on top of the dough. Then, pull the ends in opposite directions until the floss cuts all the way through the dough. Presto! Repeat in 1-inch sections.

SOUPS & SALADS

Koreans view the peach as a fruit that bestows longevity and happiness, as well as honors and riches. As one of ten immortal plants and animals, the fruit is often included in Korean folk art.

Creamy Chilled Peach Soup

INGREDIENTS

3/4 cup sour cream (or Greek yogurt)

1 cup Peach Syrup (see recipe on page 25)

1/2 cup peach juice

Fresh or canned peaches, thinly sliced and cold

Ground nutmeg or cloves (optional)

1 Whisk together the sour cream (or yogurt), peach syrup, and peach juice, or blend in a food processor. Chill for several hours before serving.

2 Garnish with peach slices. If desired, sprinkle with ground nutmeg or cloves.

Michael's Garbanzo Peach Soup

This soup goes well with many artisan breads.

1. Puree the garbanzo beans and milk.
2. Add peaches and blend well.
3. While blending, add the cinnamon, lemon juice, ginger, and sugar. Blend for two minutes.
4. Chill overnight.
5. Ladle into bowls. Garnish with a sprig of mint.

INGREDIENTS

1 can (15 ounces) garbanzo beans, rinsed and drained

1/4-1/2 cup milk (depending on desired thickness)

3 or 4 fresh, ripe peaches, peeled and diced

1/4 teaspoon cinnamon

1 1/2 tablespoons lemon juice

1/4 teaspoon ginger

2 tablespoons granulated sugar

Mint sprigs

Our friend Michael Bezas has a big smile that's as warm and wonderful as his heart. He and his wife, Cindy, a talented musician, actress, and author, live full and busy lives. Michael loves to cook—and he excels at it. I'm grateful for his willingness to create two dishes for me that celebrate peaches.

Bezas' Peach and Feta Summer Salad

INGREDIENTS

4 fresh, ripe peaches

1 small head butter lettuce

2 cups fresh baby spinach leaves

2 cups red romaine

1/2 cup crumbled feta cheese

1/4 cup walnuts, chopped

1/4 cup pine nuts

Cracked pepper

Dill weed

Dressing (see below)

1 tablespoon balsamic vinegar

2 teaspoons fresh lemon juice

2 teaspoons honey

1/4 teaspoon salt

3 tablespoons cold-pressed extra virgin olive oil

1. Peel and slice the peaches.
2. Tear the greens into bite-sized pieces, then toss and place on individual salad plates.
3. Distribute the peaches, feta, and nuts evenly on top of the salad greens.
4. Drizzle the dressing over each serving.
5. Optional: Add cracked pepper and/or sprinkle lightly with dill weed.

Dressing

1. Create the dressing by mixing together vinegar, lemon juice, honey, and salt; stir well.
2. Add the oil and blend well.

Turkey Spinach Salad

This salad is good enough for Sunday dinner, but easy enough to pack on a picnic in the park.

1. In a large bowl, toss the spinach and the almonds.
2. Place the resulting salad base on plates and dress it with chicken (or turkey) strips and peaches.
3. Drizzle with Peach Poppy Seed Vinaigrette.

INGREDIENTS

7 cups fresh baby spinach

1/2 cup toasted sliced almonds

3/4 cup cooked chicken or turkey, cut into thin strips

2 cups fresh, ripe peaches, cut into bite-sized pieces

Peach Poppy Seed Vinaigrette (see below)

Peach Poppy Seed Vinaigrette

1. Combine the peach jam, white wine vinegar, olive oil, honey, and poppy seeds in a sterile jar with a tight-fitting lid.
2. Chill for several hours.
3. Remove the jar from the refrigerator and shake well until blended.
4. Drizzle over greens and serve.

1/3 cup peach jam

1/3 cup white wine vinegar

1/4 cup olive oil

1 tablespoon honey, warmed

1 teaspoon poppy seeds

Yummy Fruit Salad

INGREDIENTS

1 large package (6 ounces) peach Jell-O

1 1/2 cups boiling water

3 ounces cream cheese, softened

1 cup diced canned peaches, well drained

1 banana, sliced

1 cup canned crushed pineapple, well drained

1 cup canned mandarin orange slices, well drained

1/2 cup pecan pieces

1 cup whipping cream

1. In a large bowl, dissolve the peach Jell-O in boiling water.
2. While water/Jell-O is still very warm, gradually add the softened cream cheese in small portions and blend with a hand mixer until smooth.
3. Chill until slightly thickened.
4. Fold in the peaches, banana, pineapple, orange slices, and pecans.
5. Beat the whipped cream until stiff, then whisk it in to the Jell-O mixture.
6. Pour into a 1 1/4 quart mold. Chill until set.

Tip: If you're in a hurry, you can soften cream cheese in the microwave for 20–30 seconds, but overheating causes scorching. The best bet is to leave it out at room temperature for at least 30 minutes prior to use.

Three Layer Tropical Salad

Layer One

INGREDIENTS

1 package (3 ounces) lemon Jell-O

1 cup boiling water

1 cup Sprite

2 cups small curd cottage cheese

1. In a medium-sized bowl, dissolve the lemon Jell-O in 1 cup boiling water.
2. Add 1 cup Sprite and chill until partly set.
3. Fold in the cottage cheese.
4. Pour the mixture into a 9 x 13-inch pan, and chill until well set.

Layer Two

1 package (3 ounces) peach Jell-O

1 cup boiling water

1 cup pineapple juice (reserved from pineapple tidbits)

1 cup diced canned peaches, well drained

1 cup canned pineapple tidbits, well drained

1. In a medium-sized bowl, dissolve the peach Jell-O in 1 cup boiling water.
2. Add the pineapple juice and chill until partly set.
3. Fold in peaches and pineapple tidbits.
4. Pour on top of first layer. Chill until well set.

Layer Three

1 package (3 ounces) pineapple Jell-O

1 cup boiling water

1 cup Sprite

1/2 package mini-marshmallows

Whipped cream topping (see below)

1. In a medium bowl, dissolve the pineapple Jell-O in 1 cup boiling water.
2. Add 1 cup Sprite. Pour on top of other layers.
3. Sprinkle in the mini-marshmallows. Chill until well set.

Topping

2-3 cups whipping cream

Cheddar cheese shreds, to taste

1. Whip cream to peaks with an electric mixer.
2. Spread over top of salad with spatula. Sprinkle with cheddar cheese.

"An apple is an excellent thing—until you have tried a peach."
—George du Maurier (1834–1896)

Peach Fluff 'n' Stuff

1. Add the cold water to a medium saucepan.
2. Stir in tapioca pudding, vanilla pudding, and Jell-O, and stir until smooth.
3. Bring the mixture to a boil, stirring constantly until mixture begins to thicken.
4. Remove the pan from the stove and allow the mixture to cool slightly.
5. Fold in the Cool Whip and peaches.
6. Chill until set.

INGREDIENTS

3 cups cold water

1 package (3 ounces) cook-and-serve tapioca pudding

1 package (3 ounces) cook-and-serve vanilla pudding

1 package (3 ounces) peach Jell-O

1 carton (8 ounces) Cool Whip

1 can (15 ounces) diced peaches, well drained

Georgia Peach Chicken Salad

Courtesy of Dickey Farms

INGREDIENTS

1/3 cup mayonnaise

2 tablespoons milk

1/2 teaspoon salt

1/4 teaspoon pepper

1 teaspoon fresh tarragon, chopped (or 1/4 teaspoon dried tarragon)

2 1/2 cups cooked chicken, cubed

1 cup seedless red grapes, halved

1 cup frozen tiny peas, thawed

2 large peaches, peeled and chopped

1 cup pecan halves, toasted

Lettuce leaves

1. In a large bowl, whisk together the mayonnaise, milk, salt, pepper, and tarragon until smooth.
2. Add the chicken; toss to coat.
3. Fold in grapes, peas, peaches, and pecans.
4. Serve in a lettuce-lined bowl.

Georgia peach production began between 1870 and 1875. At that time, there were only a few varieties that grew well in the South. A farmer could make a profit only if he could sell his crop to commercial markets in the North. At first, steamships were used to transport the fresh peaches to the Northern markets. However, rail service was much better and enhanced the chances of the peaches arriving in top condition.

Teriyaki Chicken and Peach Salad

1. In a blender or food processor, puree the peaches.
2. Add the soy sauce, ginger, brown sugar, and Tabasco. Pulse until smooth.
3. Divide the mixture in half; chill one half in the refrigerator.
4. In a large cast-iron skillet, lightly brown the tenders on both sides in olive oil.
5. Add the Sprite. Bring to a low boil.
6. Reduce heat and simmer 10 minutes, or until chicken is cooked through and tender. Discard liquid.
7. Add the first half of the peach puree mixture to the chicken.
8. Simmer thirty additional minutes.
9. Cool chicken and dice into 1/2 inch cubes.
10. Toss together cooked chicken, cabbage, diced peaches, chow mein noodles, and almonds.
11. Drizzle with the chilled portion of the peach puree mixture, or serve all ingredients wrapped in cabbage or lettuce leaves.

INGREDIENTS

2 peaches, canned

1/2 cup low-sodium soy sauce

1/2 teaspoon ground ginger

1/2 cup brown sugar

Dash of Tabasco sauce

2–3 pounds raw chicken tenders, trimmed

Olive oil

1/2 cup Sprite

1/2 head cabbage, washed and thinly sliced into short sections

Canned diced peaches

Crisp chow mein noodles

Sliced almonds

MAIN DISHES & SIDES

The phrase "You're a peach" may have originated from the tradition of giving a peach to a dear friend.

Grilled Turkey Cutlets

This tangy marinade tastes great on chicken, too.

INGREDIENTS

3/4 cup peach preserves

1/2 cup barbecue sauce

6 turkey cutlets

1. In a large bowl, mix the preserves and the barbeque sauce.
2. Pierce the turkey cutlets several times with a fork or a sharp knife.
3. Add the cutlets to the peach preserves and barbecue sauce mixture.
4. Cover bowl tightly with foil and marinate cutlets overnight in the refrigerator.
5. Remove the cutlets from the marinade and place on a heated grill.
6. Cook through (approximately 6–8 minutes), basting with remaining marinade.

Luau Coconut Grilled Shrimp and Peaches

1 In a small sauce pan, combine the brown sugar, peach juice, and butter.

2 Stir over medium heat until the butter is melted and the brown sugar is dissolved. Remove from heat.

3 In a blender, combine the almond milk, honey, one peach, and the banana. Blend until smooth. In a large bowl, combine the brown sugar mixture and the mixture from the blender. Stir until well blended.

4 Fold in the coconut. Add the shrimp and the remaining peaches and coat well.

5 Grill over low to medium heat until the shrimp is heated through.

INGREDIENTS

1 cup brown sugar

1/4 cup peach juice

1/4 cup butter

1/3 cup almond milk

1/3 cup honey

1 ripe banana

1 cup sweetened shredded coconut

3-4 pounds pre-cooked shrimp

3-4 large fresh, ripe peaches, peeled and sliced

Picking peaches on a fruit farm is fun! Search the Internet for a farm in your area and visit on a weekend. Call ahead with any questions and ask for tips. Go early in the day so you can select the best fruit. Most growers furnish picking containers, but they may charge you for them. Be careful not to pile peaches more than three or four layers deep or the peaches on the bottom will become bruised.

Ham-Stuffed Peaches

INGREDIENTS

2 ham slices, finely chopped

2 green onions, thinly sliced

2 ounces cream cheese, softened

Salt and pepper to taste

1 can (29 ounces) peach halves, drained

Buttered bread crumbs

1. Preheat oven to 350 degrees.
2. Combine ham, onions, cream cheese, and salt and pepper. Mix well.
3. Place peach halves in a greased, shallow baking dish.
4. Fill the center of the peaches with a scoop of the ham mixture.
5. Sprinkle with bread crumbs. Bake for 15 minutes.
6. Serve warm.

Grilled Sausage and Peach Skewers with Zippy Peach Marinade

INGREDIENTS

1 red onion, cut into 1/2-inch chunks

1 package turkey sausage, cut into 1/2-inch slices

1 zucchini, sliced to 1/2-inch thickness

2 fresh, ripe peaches, cut into 1/2-inch chunks

Wooden skewers

1 On wooden skewers, alternate the onion chunks with the sausage slices, zucchini, and peaches.

2 Cook on a medium-hot grill and baste with Zippy Peach Marinade until the turkey is cooked through.

Zippy Peach Marinade

1/2 cup Peach Syrup (recipe on page 25)

1/4 cup lemon juice

1 tablespoon white wine vinegar

1 tablespoon butter, melted

1 tablespoon Heinz 57 sauce

1/8 teaspoon Worcestershire Sauce

1 Whisk the marinade ingredients together.

2 Brush on skewers while grilling.

Sharon's Sunday Dinner Glazed Peaches and Pork

INGREDIENTS

1 jar (18 ounces) peach jam or preserves

1 bottle (8 ounces) Russian dressing

1 package dry Lipton Onion Soup mix

2 pounds pork loin pieces

1 can (29 ounces) sliced peaches, well drained

1. Stir together jam or preserves, Russian dressing, and soup mix.
2. Add loin pieces to Crock Pot.
3. Pour marinade over the pork and cook on medium heat for 4–5 hours; stir at least every 30 minutes. Add peaches during final hour of cooking.
4. Serve on a bed of rice.

Did you know? Columbus brought peach trees with him on his second and third voyages across the Atlantic, and Spanish missionaries first introduced peaches to America in 1571, bringing them to what is now known as St. Simon's Island, Georgia.

Georgia's Dickey Farms' Sugar 'n' Spice Grilled Peaches

INGREDIENTS

4 tablespoons butter, melted

2 teaspoons lemon juice

4 peach halves, pits removed

SUGAR MIXTURE

4 tablespoons brown sugar

1/4 teaspoon salt

1 teaspoon cinnamon

1/4 teaspoon ginger

1/8 teaspoon nutmeg

1. Stir the lemon juice into the melted butter.
2. Brush all surfaces of the peach halves with the half of the lemon-butter mixture; set aside the remaining lemon-butter.
3. Place the peaches cut side down on a grill over hot heat.
4. Grill for 3–4 minutes or until the peaches begin to brown; turn cut side up.
5. Brush the tops with the remaining lemon-butter.
6. Sprinkle with the sugar mixture; cover the grill.
7. Grill an additional 2–4 minutes, or until the peaches are soft and lightly browned.

Green Chili-Peach Sweet Pork

INGREDIENTS

5 pounds trimmed pork butt, cut into 2-inch cubes

1 teaspoon cracked black pepper

1 teaspoon cumin

1 tablespoon lime juice

1 cup water

1 cup orange juice

1 medium white onion, peeled and quartered

1. Preheat oven to 300 degrees.
2. Combine ingredients in a large cast-iron pot or Dutch oven.
3. Cover and cook in the oven for 2–3 hours, or until meat can easily be pulled apart with a fork.
4. Remove from the oven and discard all but 1/3 cup liquid.
5. On a platter, shred the pork.

Green Chili-Peach Sauce

1 small can (4 ounces) diced green chilies

2/3 cup chunky peach preserves

1/3 cup root beer

1/2 cup brown sugar

2 tablespoons Cholula Hot Sauce

1. In a medium bowl, whisk all the ingredients together.
2. Return the pork to the pot or Dutch oven. Pour sauce over pork.
3. On the stove, bring the mixture to a boil.
4. Reduce heat and simmer 10 minutes, stirring occasionally. Remove from heat.
5. Scoop pork and sauce into a 9 x 13-inch glass baking dish and spread evenly in a shallow layer.

6 Set oven to broil. Place the baking dish on the middle rack of the oven.

7 Brown mixture until it becomes bubbly and the meat begins to crisp.

8 Stir well, and repeat 2–3 times.

9 Do not overbrown or allow meat to dry out.

10 Serve on tortillas for carnitas, or on rolls or buns for barbeque.

Shiloah Baker's Peachy Keen Chicken

INGREDIENTS

1 1/2 pounds of boneless, skinless chicken breasts

Peel of one orange, zested

Juice of one orange

1 tablespoon soy sauce

1 tablespoon honey

1 1/2 teaspoons ground ginger

1 large can sliced peaches

1. Preheat the oven to 375 degrees.
2. Place all ingredients in a greased 9 x 13-inch baking dish (or stoneware dish).
3. Bake approximately 1 hour, stirring and checking the chicken every 15–20 minutes until juices run clear.

The multitalented multitasker Shiloah Baker is a military wife and mother of eight, as well as a highly successful editor and writer. Born in Panama, she has lived in Germany three times and in various places throughout the United States. Her passion for the homemaking lifestyle has impacted countless women around the globe. This recipe is her take on a deliciously quick and easy peach chicken.

Tropical Baby Carrots

1 Preheat oven to 350 degrees.

2 Cook carrots in boiling water until tender; drain.

3 Place in a buttered casserole dish.

4 Stir together pudding, coconut, and butter.

5 Drizzle the mixture over the carrots.

6 Bake for 10 minutes or until heated through.

INGREDIENTS

1 package baby carrots

1 cup Old Fashioned Peach Pudding (see recipe on page 99)

1/3 cup sweetened shredded coconut

1 tablespoon butter, melted

Sweet Mashed Sweet Potatoes

1 Preheat oven to 350 degrees.

2 Wash and peel sweet potatoes.

3 Wrap sweet potatoes in foil and bake until tender (approximately 1 hour).

4 Carefully cube hot potatoes and place them in a large bowl.

5 Add half-and-half, butter, and preserves.

6 Mash or whip until smooth.

INGREDIENTS

6 large sweet potatoes

1/4 cup nonfat half-and-half

1/4 cup butter

3 tablespoons peach preserves

Peaches 'n' Beans

INGREDIENTS

1 can (15 ounces) sliced peaches, drained

2 tablespoons reserved syrup from peaches

2 tablespoons brown sugar

Cinnamon

1 can (16 ounces) pork and beans

1. In medium skillet, stir together syrup and sugar over medium heat.
2. When sugar is dissolved, add peach slices and simmer.
3. Sprinkle with cinnamon, then stir in beans and heat through.

Did you know? The peach is one of the most popular homegrown fruits. If you want to raise your own, contact local nurseries to learn if they can be grown in your area and which varieties will thrive. The trees, which can grow 15–25 feet in height, generally begin to bear fruit at 3–4 years of age and reach their peak after a decade or so.

Peach Glazed Carrots

1. Preheat oven to 350 degrees.
2. In a medium-sized pot of water, cook carrots until tender.
3. In a small saucepan, combine water, brown sugar, and cornstarch.
4. Stirring constantly, cook sauce over medium-low heat until thickened. Stir in peaches.
5. Arrange carrots in a well-buttered baking dish.
6. Pour peach mixture over carrots, and bake covered for 10 minutes or until heated through.

INGREDIENTS

1 small package baby carrots

3/4 cup water

1/3 cup brown sugar

2 teaspoons cornstarch

1/3 cup fresh or canned peaches, pureed

Variation

1. Melt butter in saucepan.
2. Add honey, lemon juice, and peaches.
3. Add carrots and coat evenly. Bake covered for 8 minutes at 350 degrees.

2 tablespoons butter

1/2 cup honey

1 tablespoon lemon juice

1/2 cup pureed peaches

Asparagus with Peach Mock-Hollandaise

This tasty sauce is also great on turkey.

INGREDIENTS

1 pound fresh asparagus, washed and cooked until just tender

SAUCE

1/2 cup pureed fresh peach (slightly under ripe)

2 teaspoons butter, melted

1 tablespoon sour cream

1/2 teaspoon white wine vinegar

1/4 teaspoon cayenne pepper

1. Combine all ingredients for sauce in a microwave-safe bowl. Blend well. Microwave on high until heated through (30–40 seconds).

2. Stir and pour over hot asparagus or chill and pour over cooked, cooled asparagus.

Tip: The asparagus used in this dish can be steamed, boiled, grilled, sautéed, or roasted. However, take care not to overcook it, as the flavor will be diminished. One pound of asparagus is approximately 15–20 stalks. Avoid cooking asparagus in iron cookware, as the naturally occurring tannins in the vegetable will react with the iron and cause discoloration in the stalks.

A Simple Little Baked Peach

1. Preheat oven to 350 degrees.
2. Wash and peel peach. Cut in half.
3. Place halves in a small, well-greased casserole dish and prick with fork.
4. Mix lemon juice and honey together and pour over peach halves.
5. Cover and bake for 30 minutes, or until tender.
6. Serve warm or cold.

INGREDIENTS

1 fresh, ripe peach

2 teaspoons lemon juice

1/8 cup honey

A medium peach contains less than one gram of fat, which means that peaches are virtually fat free. They're also sodium free and cholesterol free. With only about 40 calories per medium peach, they're the perfect snack! My friend Phyllis loved the simple goodness of warm peaches.

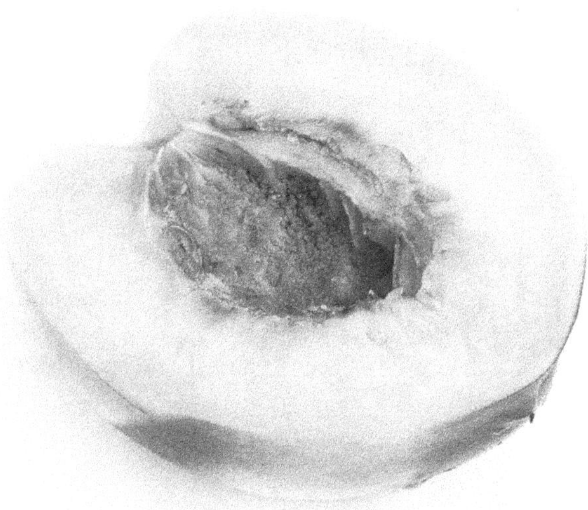

Peach and Arugula Grilled Cheese

Adapted from Macheesmo.com

INGREDIENTS

Butter

4 slices ciabatta or sourdough bread

2 very ripe peaches, sliced thin

4–6 ounces Gruyère cheese, sliced

Arugula

1. Butter both sides of bread slices.
2. Heat large nonstick skillet over medium-low heat. Place one or two bread slices in pan.
3. Add one layer each of peaches and Gruyère.
4. Top with a few leaves of arugula and bread slice or slices.
5. When the cheese begins to soften, flip the sandwich with a spatula and continue cooking until cheese is bubbly. (It's better to flip the sandwiches a few times than to overbrown or burn the bread before the cheese melts.)

Cheesy Peaches

INGREDIENTS

1/2 cup cottage cheese

2 teaspoons honey

6 fresh or canned peach halves

Cinnamon

1. Combine cottage cheese and honey. Spoon into peach halves.
2. Sprinkle with cinnamon.
3. Chill well, and serve cold or bake at 350 degrees for 15 minutes.

BREADS, MUFFINS & CUPCAKES

One medium peach provides more than 10 percent of your daily requirement of Vitamin A and almost 20 percent for Vitamin C.

Because the fresh season is so short, California Cling Peaches harvested during the summer are handpicked at the peak of flavor and ripeness and preserved at the cannery within hours to seal in the flavor and nutrients for use all year.

Reminiscent of comfort foods from the past, Rise and Shine California Cling Peach Scones are flaky (thanks to the buttermilk) while serving up a subtly sweet flavor. You can choose to add a touch of cinnamon. Warm from the oven, these biscuit-like wonders are sure to make your family and friends "rise and shine."

Rise and Shine California Cling Peach Scones

Courtesy of the California Cling Peach Board

INGREDIENTS

3 cups + 3 tablespoons flour

3/4 cup granulated sugar

5 teaspoons baking powder

1/2 teaspoon baking soda

1/4 teaspoon cinnamon (optional)

1/2 cup butter, diced into small pieces

1/2 teaspoon vanilla extract

1 egg

1/2 cup buttermilk

1 can California Cling Peaches, drained and diced

1 Preheat oven to 375 degrees.

2 Mix scone ingredients (in order listed) in a KitchenAid mixer or using a hand pastry mixer.

3 Add the buttermilk slowly, just enough to allow the mixture to form a dough without making it too wet. If you need more buttermilk to moisten the dough, add it only a tablespoon at a time. Be careful not to overwork as the dough will become tough.

4 Hand-form scones into rounds and press or lightly roll each round to a 1-inch thickness. Cut into triangles with a pizza cutter. Place the triangles on a cookie sheet covered with parchment paper.

5 Bake scones for 22 minutes, or until light brown on the bottom.

6 Mix the glaze and brush it onto the scones with a pastry brush, or drizzle on with a spoon.

GLAZE

1/3 cup powdered sugar

2 tablespoons milk

Makes 10–12 medium-sized scones or 16–20 miniscones.

Oatmeal Peach Bread

1 Preheat oven to 350 degrees.

2 Beat together eggs, oil, and sugar.

3 Add peaches and mix well.

4 Combine dry ingredients and add to peach mixture. Stir until well blended.

5 Pour into a large, greased loaf pan.

6 Bake 50 minutes or until center is done.

INGREDIENTS

2 eggs

1/3 cup oil

1/2 cup brown sugar

1 cup fresh or canned peaches, pureed

1 1/2 cups flour

1 teaspoon baking soda

1 teaspoon baking powder

1 teaspoon cinnamon

1/2 teaspoon nutmeg

1 cup quick oats

1/2 cup walnuts (optional)

Peach Zucchini Bread

This sweet bread is a perennial Brigham City, Utah favorite!

INGREDIENTS

1 cup oil

2 cups granulated sugar

3 eggs

1 cup zucchini, shredded

1 cup fresh or canned peaches, diced

3 cups flour

1 teaspoon baking soda

1 teaspoon baking powder

1. Preheat oven to 325 degrees.
2. Beat oil, sugar, and eggs together.
3. Stir in zucchini and peaches, and mix well.
4. Slowly stir in dry ingredients.
5. Bake for 60 minutes or until toothpick inserted in center of loaves comes out clean.

It's a running joke and a baffling mystery: what do you do with excess zucchini? Or, in other words, how fast can you run after you've dropped off a load of zucchini on your neighbor's front porch? Zucchini seems to multiply in the garden much faster that it can ever be consumed. However, my all-time favorite way to make use of it is in sweet bread. I adapted a family recipe to incorporate peaches and am pleased that our chamber of commerce considers it a local favorite.

Old-Fashioned Peach Bread

1. Preheat oven to 350 degrees.
2. Cream together sugar, butter, and eggs.
3. Add sour cream and peaches, then add baking soda, spices, flour, and nuts.
4. Bake in a well-greased loaf pan until center is firm.

INGREDIENTS

1 cup granulated sugar

1/3 cup butter

3 eggs

3 tablespoons sour cream

1 cup fresh peaches, diced

1 teaspoon baking soda

1 teaspoon allspice

1 teaspoon cinnamon

1 teaspoon nutmeg

1 teaspoon ground cloves

2 cups flour

1 cup slivered almonds or pecan halves

Quick Oatmeal Peachies

INGREDIENTS

1 box (7 ounces) Jiffy Oatmeal Muffin Mix

1/3 cup fresh or frozen peaches, pureed

1 egg

1/4 cup pecans, chopped

1. Prepare muffin mix according to package directions, except substitute peach puree for milk.
2. Fold in pecans.
3. Bake according to package directions.

Did you know? Peaches, along with apricots, plums, and cherries, are members of the rose family. Peach blossom petals, which taste faintly like almonds, can be used as a garnish for foods and drinks—however, make sure they have been grown organically and use sparingly, as too many can cause an upset stomach. Bouquets of peach blossoms are carried by Chinese brides.

Honeyville Farms' Spiced Buttermilk Peach Carrot Crumb Cakes with Maple-Hazelnut Glaze

Courtesy of Chef Stephanie Petersen, www.cheftessbakeresse.com

INGREDIENTS

1 1/2 cups Honeyville freeze dried peaches

1/2 cup Honeyville dehydrated carrots

1 1/4 cups boiling water

3/4 cup vegetable oil

3/4 cup granulated sugar

3/4 cup Honeyville 6-grain steam rolled mix

1 tablespoon Chef Tess Wise Women of the East Spice OR 2 tablespoons Saigon cinnamon + 1 teaspoon pumpkin pie spice

2 teaspoons pure vanilla extract

4 large eggs

2 3/4 cups Honeyville buttermilk pancake mix

1. Preheat oven to 350 degrees. Line 24 muffin tins with paper liners.
2. In a glass or metal medium-sized bowl, combine the freeze-dried peaches and dehydrated carrots with boiling water.
3. Set aside, and let them hydrate for 10 minutes.
4. In the meantime, combine the vegetable oil, sugar, 6-grain rolled mix, Chef Tess spices blend, vanilla, eggs, and zest of one orange in a large bowl.
5. Add the undrained peaches and carrots mixture and the pancake mix.
6. Beat by hand 100 strokes.
7. Fill 24 muffin cups 3/4 full.

Streusel Crumb Cake Topping

- 1/2 cup melted butter (no substitutions)
- 2 1/3 cups Honeyville Buttermilk pancake mix
- 2/3 cup granulated sugar
- 2 teaspoons Chef Tess Wise Women of the East Spice and Floral Blend

1. Combine the melted butter with the dry ingredients until chunky-crumbly.
2. Generously top your cakes with the topping and bake at 350 degrees for 15–18 minutes.

Maple-Hazelnut Glaze

- 1/4 cup honey
- 1/4 teaspoon maple extract
- 1/3 cup hazelnuts, pulverized
- 1 tablespoon boiling water
- 1 cup powdered sugar

1. Combine all ingredients until smooth.
2. Drizzle over warm muffins.

Where is that peach orchard, do you know?
Where all those perfect peaches grow.
The trees must be fruitful for year after year,
As the ripe peaches drop off, new buds appear.

—1912 postcard

Easy Cran-Peach Cornbread Muffins

1 Mix together cornbread mix, egg, and yogurt (substitute yogurt for 1/3 cup milk on package directions).

2 Fold in peaches and Craisins or cranberries.

3 Bake according to package directions.

Makes 6–8 muffins.

INGREDIENTS

1 box (8.5 ounces) Jiffy corn bread mix

1 egg, beaten

1/3 cup vanilla yogurt

1/4 cup fresh or canned peaches, chopped

1/4 cup cherry Craisins or dried cranberries

Peach Cupcakes for Monica

INGREDIENTS

1/2 stick unsalted butter, room temperature

2 ounces cream cheese, room temperature

1 cup granulated sugar

3 large eggs

2 tablespoons peach preserves

1/2 cup buttermilk

1/4 cup Welch's White Grape Peach Juice

1 1/2 cups cake flour, sifted

1 teaspoon baking powder

1/2 teaspoon vanilla

Frosting (see opposite page)

1. Preheat oven to 350 degrees.
2. Cream together butter, cream cheese, and sugar. Beat in eggs.
3. Add peach preserves, buttermilk, and juice. Blend.
4. Slowly add dry ingredients. Beat on low just until blended.
5. Bake for 16–18 minutes. Cool before frosting.

Did you know? The "World's Largest Peach" is actually a water tower built in the shape of a peach. Located in Gaffney, South Carolina, this giant peach—The Peachoid—weighs over 10,000 pounds.

Frosting

1 Beat cream cheese on medium until creamy. Gradually add in butter and beat until fluffy.

2 Add peach preserves and juice and beat one minute on low.

3 Gradually add powdered sugar, 1/4 cup at a time, and beat just until uniform and smooth. Do not overbeat. Spread generously over cooled cupcakes.

4 ounces cream cheese, room temperature

1/2 stick butter, room temperature

1 tablespoon peach preserves, room temperature

1 tablespoon Welch's White Grape Peach Juice, room temperature

1 1/2-2 cups powdered sugar

Low-Fat Peach Cupcakes

INGREDIENTS

2 eggs

2 cups Greek peach yogurt

1/2 cup low-sugar peach juice, reserved from canned peaches

1/2 teaspoon vanilla

1/2 teaspoon lemon extract

1 package yellow cake mix

1/2 cup canned diced low-sugar peaches

1. Preheat oven according to cake mix package directions.
2. Beat eggs. Whisk in yogurt, peach juice, vanilla, and lemon extract.
3. Add cake mix. Beat according to package directions until combined. Fold in peaches.
4. Pour into liners in muffin tins.
5. Bake according to package directions, about 20–22 minutes or until toothpick inserted in center comes out clean.

Topping

1 cup low-fat whipping cream

Peach dices

1. Whip cream until soft peaks form.
2. Top with peach dices.

PIES & CAKES

Because of their pits, peaches are sometimes referred to as stone fruit.

Peach Cream Cheese Pie

INGREDIENTS

1 package (8 ounces) cream cheese, room temperature

3/4 cup powdered sugar

1 teaspoon vanilla

1 cup whipping cream OR Cool Whip, thawed

1 pie shell, graham cracker crust OR baked pie crust, cooled

1 cup prepared peach pie filling, chilled

1. Combine cream cheese, sugar, and vanilla.
2. Whip cream, then fold into cream cheese mixture. Blend thoroughly. Pour into pie shell.
3. Top with peach pie filling, and chill well before serving.

Baby Pies

INGREDIENTS

6 premade miniature graham cracker crusts

1 package (3 ounces) vanilla pudding

Fresh peaches

1. Prepare pudding according to package directions.
2. Divide between crusts.
3. Top with fresh peach slices.

Peach of a Pecan Pie

1. Preheat oven to 375 degrees.
2. Whisk together pudding and corn syrup.
3. Gradually whisk in milk, preserves, and eggs. Fold in pecans.
4. Pour into pie shells and bake until top is firm (about 40 minutes). Cool completely.
5. Garnish with whipped cream (or vanilla ice cream) and peaches.

INGREDIENTS

1 package (3 ounces) instant vanilla pudding

1 cup dark corn syrup

3/4 cup sweetened condensed milk

1/2 cup peach preserves

4 eggs, beaten

1 1/2 cups pecans, chopped

2 (8-inch) pie shells, unbaked

Whipped cream OR vanilla ice cream

Fresh, ripe peaches, sliced

Brigham City Peach Jumble Pie

INGREDIENTS

2 cups fresh rhubarb stalks, sliced lengthwise into halves or thirds and then cut into 1-inch sections

2/3 cup-1 cup granulated sugar

1 cup water

1 package (3 ounces) strawberry-kiwi flavored Jell-O

2 cups canned peaches, cut into bite-sized pieces

2 cups fresh strawberries, sliced into quarters

1. Place rhubarb in a medium sauce pan with sugar and water.
2. Stir until sugar is dissolved and bring to a boil over medium heat. Reduce heat.
3. Stew rhubarb until just tender, about 3–5 minutes.
4. Stir in Jell-O until dissolved. Remove from heat.
5. Allow to cool slightly before adding peaches and strawberries.
6. Pour mixture into two 9-inch pie plates.
7. Chill overnight or until firmly set.

How much sugar do you need to tame the sourness of rhubarb in order to make it a palatable partner for other fruits? In this recipe, I use 1/3 cup sugar for each cup of rhubarb. I sometimes even add an extra 1/3 cup of sugar to help carry the other two fruits in this pie—strawberries and peaches. That way, if they, too, are a bit on the tart side, they get an extra boost of sweetness. Depending on the ripeness and quality of the fruits you have available, start out with a lesser amount and add more if you need to.

Topping

1 cup peach juice

2 tablespoons flour

1/4 cup powdered sugar

1/3 cup granulated sugar

1 egg, well beaten

1/2 pint whipping cream

2 tablespoons wheat germ

1. Over medium heat, stir together juice, flour, sugars, and egg until smooth.
2. Stirring constantly, bring to a boil. Boil one minute or until thickened.
3. Remove and cool thoroughly.
4. Whip the cream and fold into cooled mixture.
5. Divide and spread over both pies.
6. Sprinkle each pie with 1 tablespoon wheat germ.

Rhubarb, a vegetable, is often referred to as the "pie plant" because it is most commonly used as a filling for pies. The leaves of the plant are not edible; they contain oxalic acid and are highly toxic. Use only fresh, high-quality rhubarb that is crisp and blemish free. To prepare, wash the stalks well and remove root ends and leaves. If the rhubarb is stringy or fibrous, cut just beneath the skin on the root end and pull the strings away down the length of the stalk.

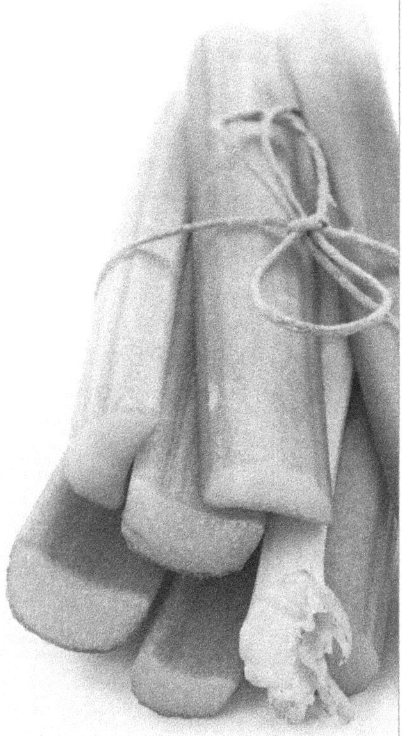

Famous Idle Isle Peach Pie

INGREDIENTS

2 cups fresh peaches, sliced

1 cup fresh peaches, mashed

1 cup granulated sugar

3 tablespoons cornstarch

1/2 cup orange juice

1 baked pie shell

1. Whisk sugar and cornstarch together and set aside.
2. Combine orange juice and mashed peaches in a saucepan and bring to a boil.
3. Slowly whisk in sugar/cornstarch mixture. Return to a boil.
4. Turn to low and let mixture simmer for about 5 minutes.
5. Cool, then add sliced peaches and pour into pie shell.
6. Top with whipping cream or ice cream.

Melt-in-your-mouth dinner rolls. Savory pot roast and mashed potatoes. Turkey with sage dressing. And, oh, the idle berry pie! A match made in heaven, the blueberries and marionberries in Idle Isle Cafe's idle berry pie bring customers from all over the country. But on Peach Days it's all about the peaches, and this historic Brigham City cafe offers up a pie that converts even staunch berry-lovers into peach aficionados.

Fran's Peach Pie

1. Preheat oven to 425 degrees.
2. Combine sugar, flour, cinnamon, and peaches. Mix well to coat peaches.
3. Place in pie shell. Arrange the butter sections on top of the peaches.
4. Top with pie crust; cut slits in top. Brush top with milk and sprinkle lightly with sugar.
5. Bake for 35–45 minutes.

INGREDIENTS

1 1/2 cups granulated sugar

1/3 cup flour

1/2 teaspoon cinnamon

4 cups fresh peaches, sliced

1 prepared pie shell, unbaked

1/4 stick butter, cut into thin (1/8-inch) sections

1 prepared pie crust, unbaked

Milk

Granulated sugar

My mother-in-law spent the majority of her life as a single mom to three very active boys, so she had to learn to live on a tight shoe-string budget. Nonetheless, my husband and his brothers quickly attest that she kept them well fed. Tasty mainstays from their childhood include savory soups, her much-in-demand lasagna, meatballs, and Polish sausage, and an abundant variety of cookies. Fran is indeed a fabulous cook, and I'm grateful for all I've learned from her—in life and cooking. With this pie, she cautions that if the edges seem to brown too fast, you should protect them with strips of tinfoil.

Grandma's Special White Cake with Peaches and Cream

INGREDIENTS

1/2 cup shortening

1 cup granulated sugar

2 eggs

1 tablespoon vanilla

2 cups cake flour

1/2 teaspoon salt

3 teaspoons baking powder

1 cup milk

Whipped cream, sweetened

Fresh, ripe peaches

Mint sprigs

1. Preheat oven to 350 degrees.
2. Cream together shortening, sugar, and eggs. Stir in vanilla.
3. Sift flour, salt, and baking powder together.
4. Alternately add dry ingredients and milk to shortening mixture. Batter will be thick.
5. Pour into two 9-inch round, greased layer pans.
6. Bake for about 30 minutes.
7. When cooled, fill and top with sweetened whipped cream.
8. Garnish with fresh peaches and mint sprigs.

I obtained this recipe from a friend in Iowa—though I never discovered whose grandmother to attribute it to. A few years ago, a regional newspaper decided to use this recipe for a fall column featuring peaches. The result was, well, beautiful. Artistically arranged by one of their cooking staffers, the fresh peach slices on a backdrop of white whipped cream was stunning. I'm sure they had as much fun eating the cake as they did making it!

Peach Cake

1. Preheat oven to 350 degrees.
2. Dissolve Jell-O in water. Add eggs and beat 2–3 minutes.
3. Add cake mix and pureed peaches and beat 2 minutes more.
4. Bake in a greased 9 x 13-inch pan for 40 minutes.
5. Remove from oven when center is done.
6. While still hot, prick holes in cake with a fork.
7. Mix peach juice and powdered sugar together until smooth and spread over hot cake.
8. Garnish with fresh peach slices.

INGREDIENTS

1 package (3 ounces) peach Jell-O

3/4 cup boiling water

4 eggs

2 boxes butter pecan cake mix

3/4 cup canned peaches, pureed

1/2 cup peach juice

2 cups powdered sugar

Fresh peach slices

Gingerbread Upside-Down Peach Cake

INGREDIENTS

2 tablespoons butter or margarine

1/4 cup corn syrup

1/4 cup brown sugar

1 can (15 ounces) sliced peaches, drained

1/2 cup macadamia nuts

1/3 cup butter or shortening

1/2 cup granulated sugar

1 beaten egg

2/3 cup light molasses

2 cups flour

2 teaspoons baking powder

1/4 teaspoon baking soda

1 teaspoon cinnamon

2 teaspoons ginger

3/4 cup milk

1. Preheat oven to 350 degrees.
2. Melt butter in a 7 x 11-inch rectangular cake pan.
3. Pour in syrup and add brown sugar; blend.
4. Arrange peach slices in pan.
5. Sprinkle nuts evenly on top of peaches.

Gingerbread

6. Cream butter (or shortening) and sugar.
7. Add egg; beat thoroughly.
8. Add molasses. Beat.
9. Alternately add sifted dry ingredients and milk.
10. Pour batter over peach slices.
11. Bake for 40 minutes or until done. When cooled, invert on a platter to cut.

Gingerbread Upside-Down Peach Cake is wonderful topped with freshly whipped cream and served with a cup of warm apple cider. You can use either fresh or canned peaches. If you use fresh and they're a little tart, bump up the brown sugar to 1/2 cup instead of the 1/4 you would use for canned peaches.

Cream Cheese Peach Cake

1. Preheat oven to 350 degrees.
2. Combine flour, baking powder, egg, pudding, butter, and milk in a mixing bowl.
3. Beat 2 minutes at moderate speed.
4. Pour into a greased 9-inch round pan. Top batter with sliced peaches.
5. In a separate bowl, cream together cream cheese, sugar, and reserved juice.
6. Spoon cream cheese mixture over batter, staying 1 inch away from sides.
7. Bake for 30–36 minutes or until the crust is golden brown. Filling will appear soft.
8. Store in refrigerator.

INGREDIENTS

3/4 cup flour

1 teaspoon baking powder

1 egg

1 package (3 ounces) cook vanilla pudding (not instant)

3 tablespoons butter, softened

1/2 cup milk

1 can (15 ounces) sliced peaches, drained; reserve juice

1 package (8 ounces) cream cheese

1/2 cup granulated sugar

3 tablespoons reserved peach juice

Minnie's Peach Glacé Cake

INGREDIENTS

2 cups cake flour

1 1/2 cups sugar

3 1/2 teaspoons baking powder

1 teaspoon salt

1/2 cup shortening (half soft butter, if desired)

1 cup whole milk

1 teaspoon vanilla

3 eggs, beaten

1. Heat oven to 350 degrees.
2. Grease and flour 2 round layer pans.
3. In a large mixer bowl, combine all the ingredients. Blend on low for 30 seconds, scraping sides and bottom of bowl.
4. Beat 3 minutes on medium, scraping bowl frequently.
5. Pour into prepared pans.
6. Bake for 35–40 minutes or until toothpick inserted in center comes out clean. Cool.

Peach Glacé

1 package (12 ounces) frozen sliced peaches, OR 3-4 fresh, ripe peaches.

2 teaspoons cornstarch

1. Thaw and drain peaches, reserving syrup.
2. Mix syrup with cornstarch.
3. Cook over medium heat, stirring constantly until mixture thickens and boils.
4. Boil 1 minute. Remove from heat and cool.
5. Arrange half of the peach slices on top of one of the cake layers.
6. Carefully spread glacé over fruit with a

small brush or spoon. Add a few drops of water if glacé is too thick.

Filling

1 1/2 cups whipping cream, chilled

1/3 cup confectioner's sugar

Peach slices

1. In a medium bowl, whip chilled whipping cream and confectioner's sugar until stiff.
2. Chop remaining peaches coarsely; fold into 1 cup of the whipped cream mixture.
3. Fill layers, placing glacéd fruit layer on top.
4. Frost sides of cake with remaining whipped cream mixture. Chill before serving.

My maternal grandmother, Minnie, loved to collect recipes. At one time, she and my Aunt Janie were cooks at a local hunting club. Then referred to as the Million Dollar Duck Club, the establishment hosted such notables as Andy Devine and Art Linkletter. In fact, Grandma once baked a special chocolate cake for Mr. Linkletter's birthday. Though the preceding recipe is very similar to Grandma's Special White Cake with Peaches and Cream, the glacé and filling make this cake unique, and I include it in honor of my own grandmother.

COOKIES & COBBLERS

President Thomas Jefferson regarded the peach as a fancy delicacy for the table. While George Washington's Mount Vernon orchard had only two specific varieties of peaches, in Monticello, Jefferson cultivated over thirty-eight varieties in his South Orchard alone. In his book, The Fruit and Fruit Trees of Monticello, *Peter J. Hatch notes, "The peach was the queen bee, the workhorse of tree fruits at Monticello; a luxury because of its abundance, its usefulness, but also, simply, because Thomas Jefferson liked peaches." From 1977 to 2012, Hatch served as Director of Gardens and Grounds at Monticello, Virginia, where he oversaw maintenance, interpretation, and conservation, meticulously restoring Jefferson's 2,400 acre landscape—including the peach trees.*

Individual Peachy Pizzas

INGREDIENTS

1 (16 ounce) package refrigerated sugar cookie dough

1 fresh or canned peach

1. Preheat oven according to sugar cookie dough package directions.
2. Slice or roll dough into balls for 12 large cookies.
3. Bake according to package directions.
4. Slice peach into 12 slices.

Topping

2 tablespoons Peach Syrup (see recipe on page 25) OR peach juice

1 teaspoon vanilla extract

2 tablespoons instant vanilla pudding

4 ounces cream cheese, softened

1/2 cup powdered sugar

Fresh blueberries and/or raspberries

5. While cookies are baking, stir together peach syrup (or peach juice) and vanilla extract in a small bowl.
6. Add vanilla pudding and stir until smooth.
7. Blend in cream cheese and powdered sugar and whip until smooth.
8. Topping can be served on hot or cooled cookies. If served hot, top with slice of peach and sprinkle with cinnamon. If served on cooled cookies, chop peach slice into eight sections and place on topping with blueberries or raspberries.

Peach Dainties

INGREDIENTS

2 cups all-purpose flour

2 teaspoons granulated sugar

1 cup butter

1 package (8 ounces) cream cheese

Peach jam

Brown sugar

Chopped nuts

1. Preheat oven to 375 degrees.
2. In a large bowl, mix flour and sugar.
3. Cut butter and cream cheese into flour mixture until coarse and crumbly.
4. Knead into a ball; chill 1 hour.
5. Remove dough from refrigerator. Roll out on ungreased cookie sheet to edges.
6. Bake for 10–15 minutes, or until edges start to brown. Remove from oven.
7. While still warm, spread jam over surface and cut into 1 1/2-inch squares.
8. Sprinkle with brown sugar and nuts.

Peach Coconut Chews

INGREDIENTS

1/2 cup Peach Syrup (see recipe on page 25)

1 cup powdered sugar

1 teaspoon vanilla

1/4 teaspoon almond extract

1/2 cup pecans

1 cup dried peaches, chopped

1. Stir together syrup and sugar in a small saucepan.
2. Bring to a boil, stirring constantly. Boil 1 minute. Remove from heat.
3. Stir in vanilla, almond extract, pecans, and peaches.
4. Drop by spoonfuls onto waxed paper and allow to cool.

Peach Snickerdoodles

INGREDIENTS

1 cup shortening, softened

1 1/2 cups granulated sugar

2 eggs

2 3/4 cups flour, sifted

2 teaspoons cream of tartar

1 teaspoon baking soda

1/4 teaspoon salt

2 tablespoons dried peaches, finely minced

2 tablespoons brown sugar

2 teaspoons cinnamon

1. Preheat oven to 400 degrees.
2. Cream shortening, sugar, and eggs.
3. Sift dry ingredients together, then slowly add to shortening mixture.
4. Roll dough into balls the size of small walnuts.
5. Combine peaches, brown sugar, and cinnamon; coat balls in dry mixture.
6. Place 2 inches apart on an ungreased baking sheet.
7. Bake for 8–10 minutes or until lightly browned but still soft.

Esther's Cobbler

INGREDIENTS

1/2 cup flour

1/2 teaspoon baking powder

2 tablespoons butter, softened

1/2 cup granulated sugar

1/2 teaspoon salt

1 large egg, slightly beaten

Fresh peaches or peach pie filling

1. Preheat oven to 350 degrees.
2. Combine flour, baking powder, butter, sugar, salt, and the egg and beat until smooth. Set aside.
3. Cover bottom of greased cake pan with sliced peaches or peach pie filling.
4. Heat in 350-degree oven until peaches are hot. Remove from oven.
5. Drop flour mixture by spoonfuls over hot fruit. Dough will spread as it bakes.
6. Bake for approximately 30 minutes or until golden brown.

My paternal grandmother, Esther, loved to cook just as much as my Grandma Minnie. While she never cooked for celebrities, she turned out simple, homemade dishes that were welcome mainstays on her and my grandfather's small Idaho farm. Served with a side of her wit and wisdom, Grandma's delicious meals filled many stomachs while warming both heart and soul.

Every year on Peach Days, tens of thousands of visitors flock to Brigham City to partake of local hospitality and taste the home-grown fare. At the Main Street food courts, dozens of Dutch ovens brimming with piping hot peach cobbler fill the air with the most tantalizing aroma. Top off a dish of cobbler with a generous scoop of vanilla ice cream, and it's no wonder people wait in line for hours for the stuff. My fond memories of Peach Days, strolling down Main Street sharing a bowl of cobbler and a bag of hot caramel corn from the Capitol Theatre with my husband, convinced me to try a recipe that combined the flavors of both. Whether it's my version of peach cobbler, or just the sauce drizzled over a grilled peach, I think warm peaches and caramel bring out the best in each other.

Caramel Cobbler

INGREDIENTS

1 tablespoon butter

2 cans (29 ounces each) peach slices

1 box (16 ounces) pound cake mix

1 cup Keebler Pecan Sandies cookies, crumbed

1. Preheat oven according to pound cake mix directions.
2. In 9 x 13-inch pan, melt butter. Spread over bottom of pan.
3. Arrange peach slices in butter.
4. Mix pound cake according to package directions and fold in Pecan Sandies.
5. Pour cake batter over peaches. Bake according to pound cake mix directions.
6. Top with caramel sauce.

Caramel Sauce

1. Combine all ingredients in small pan and stir over medium heat until sugar is dissolved. Bring to a low boil.
2. Remove from heat and drizzle over cobbler.
3. Don't forget the vanilla ice cream!

1/2 cup evaporated milk

1/2 cup butter

1/2 cup brown sugar

1 teaspoon vanilla

Fast Peach Cobbler

1. Preheat oven to 325 degrees.
2. Place peaches in bottom of greased cake pan. Sprinkle with dry cake mix.
3. Pour butter and reserved syrup evenly over cake mix.
4. Bake for 1 hour or until done.

INGREDIENTS

1 can (29 ounces) sliced peaches, reserve syrup

1 box yellow cake mix

1/2 cup butter or margarine, melted

(Photo courtesy Brigham City Chamber of Commerce.)

Spiced Peach Cookies

INGREDIENTS

1 (16 ounce) package refrigerated sugar cookie dough

1 batch Spiced Peach Refrigerator Jam (see recipe on page 124)

1. Preheat oven according to cookie dough package directions.
2. Roll dough into balls and place on cookie sheet.
3. Depress center of each ball with a spoon, creating a deep hollow, and fill with 1 teaspoon of Spiced Peach Jam.
4. Bake according to package directions. Add 1–2 minutes to baking time if centers seem too doughy.

DESSERTS

There are some 700 varieties of peaches. One hundred to two hundred different cultivars (cultivated varieties) are grown in the United States. See page 131 for characteristics and uses of the most popular peach varieties.

Peach Custard Divine

INGREDIENTS

1 tablespoon butter, melted

1 1/4 cup flour, sifted

1/2 cup + 1 tablespoon granulated sugar

3 tablespoons butter, room temperature

1 can (15 ounces) sliced peaches, well drained (reserve 1/2 cup juice)

1/2 teaspoon cinnamon

1 cup evaporated milk

1 egg, well beaten

1/4 cup sliced almonds (optional)

1-2 tablespoons candied ginger, grated (optional)

1. Preheat oven to 375 degrees.
2. Brush sides of 8-inch square baking dish with melted butter. Mix flour, 1 tablespoon sugar, and room temperature butter with a pastry blender until mixture resembles coarse meal.
3. Press dough firmly onto the bottom and halfway up the sides of the baking dish. Ensure mixture is distributed evenly.
4. Arrange peaches on top of dough. Sprinkle with cinnamon.
5. Bake for 20 minutes.
6. Combine evaporated milk, reserved peach juice, and the remaining 1/2 cup sugar; stir until sugar is dissolved. Whisk in egg; pour mixture over the top of the peaches.
7. Bake for 30 more minutes, or until set.
8. Chill well. Sprinkle almonds and optional ginger over custard and serve cold.

Tangy Peach Pudding

1. For cold pudding, use instant pudding mix. For hot pudding, use cook-and-serve mix.
2. Prepare pudding according to package directions.
3. Stir in Spiced Peach Jam.
4. Top with peach slices.

INGREDIENTS

1 small package (3 ounces) vanilla instant pudding

OR

1 small package (3 ounces) vanilla cook-and-serve pudding

1 batch Spiced Peach Refrigerator Jam (recipe on page 124)

Old-Fashioned Peach Pudding

1. In a small saucepan, stir water and sugar over medium heat until sugar is dissolved.
2. Whisk in cornstarch and bring to a boil, stirring constantly. Boil gently until thickened.
3. Add pureed peaches and vanilla and simmer 1 minute. Chill well before serving.

INGREDIENTS

3/4 cup water

3/4 cup brown sugar

2 teaspoons cornstarch

1 cup fresh or canned peaches, pureed

1 teaspoon vanilla

Peaches and Chips with Cinnamon Sauce

INGREDIENTS

1 sheet frozen puff pastry dough, thawed at room temperature 30-40 minutes or until easy to handle

Fresh, ripe peaches, peeled and sliced

Vanilla ice cream

1. Preheat oven according to pastry dough package directions.
2. Lay out pastry dough on lightly greased cookie sheet. With a pizza cutter, cut into triangles (about the size of a tortilla chip) and separate.
3. Bake according to package directions or until puffed and golden brown.
4. Serve warm with peaches and vanilla ice cream. Top with cinnamon sauce.

Cinnamon Sauce

1/2 cup honey

1/4 cup peach juice

1 cup powdered sugar

1 cup Peach Syrup (see recipe on page 25)

1 teaspoon cinnamon

1. In a small pan, combine honey, peach juice, and powdered sugar. Stir until sugar is dissolved.
2. Stir in peach syrup and cinnamon and blend well.
3. Serve hot on Peaches and Chips.

This sauce is also great on rolls, pancakes, or muffins.

Peach Sorbet

1. In a medium saucepan, bring sugar and water to a boil, stirring constantly.
2. Add pureed peaches and boil 1 minute.
3. Whisk in lemon juice and pour mixture into a freezer-safe container; freeze until solid, or freeze in ice cube trays (see A Peachy Summer Lemonade and Peach Blueberry Blast recipes on pages 14 and 15).

INGREDIENTS

1 cup granulated sugar

1/2 cup water

2 cups pureed fresh or canned peaches

2-4 tablespoons lemon juice

Peach Squares

INGREDIENTS

2 sheets frozen puff pastry dough, thawed at room temperature 30–40 minutes or until easy to handle

1 package (8 ounces) cream cheese, softened

1 teaspoon vanilla

1/2 cup powdered sugar

1 egg, beaten

Fresh or canned peach slices

1/2 cup Cinnamon Sauce (see recipe on page 100)

Powdered sugar (optional)

1. Preheat oven according to pastry dough directions.
2. Place first pastry sheet into bottom of lightly greased 9-inch square pan.
3. Bake according to package directions until just puffed and light golden brown. Remove from oven.
4. Blend together cream cheese, vanilla, powdered sugar, and egg. Carefully spread on top of baked pastry.
5. Top with peach slices and drizzle with 1/4 cup cinnamon sauce.
6. Lay out second pastry sheet on top of peaches. Drizzle with remaining sauce.
7. Bake at 350 for 30–35 minutes or until pastry is golden brown.
8. Cool and cut into squares.
9. If desired, sprinkle with powdered sugar.

Raspberry Peach Supreme

1. Preheat oven to 350 degrees.
2. In food processor, crumb cookies. Mix 1 cup crumbs with 1/4 cup melted butter and press into bottom of 8-inch square pan.
3. Cream together 1/2 cup softened butter and sugar.
4. Add eggs, one at a time, and beat well after each addition.
5. Pour mixture over crumbs. Sprinkle with chopped walnuts.
6. Bake for 20–30 minutes, or until center is firm.
7. Chill thoroughly. Before serving, top with peaches, raspberries, and whipped cream. Sprinkle with remaining crumbs.

INGREDIENTS

1 1/2 cups butter cookies, crumbed

1/4 cup butter, melted

1/2 cup butter, softened

1 cup powdered sugar

2 eggs

1/3 cup chopped walnuts

2 cups fresh peaches, sliced

2 cups fresh raspberries

1 cup whipping cream, whipped

Peach Shorties

1. Wash, peel, and pit peaches.
2. Slice peaches and divide between shortcake cups or cake slices.
3. Top with whipped cream.

INGREDIENTS

Fresh, ripe peaches

Shortcake cups or sliced pound cake

Whipped Cream

Easy Peach Melba

INGREDIENTS

Vanilla ice cream

Fresh, ripe peach halves, pits and peels removed

Raspberry jam, warmed

1. Place one scoop of ice cream in each peach half.
2. Pour raspberry jam over top.

Peach Tapioca

INGREDIENTS

2 1/4 cups milk

1/2 cup peach juice

1/2 cup granulated sugar

1 egg, beaten

3 tablespoons Kraft Minute Quick Cooking Tapioca

1 teaspoon vanilla

1/2 cup diced fresh peaches

1. Mix milk, peach juice, sugar, egg, and tapioca together in a small saucepan, and let stand 5 minutes.
2. Over medium heat, stir constantly and bring mixture to a full boil. Remove from heat.
3. Stir in vanilla and peaches; chill.

"The ripest peach is highest on the tree."

—James Whitcomb Riley (1849-1916)

Harvest Trifle

1. Preheat oven according to spice cake mix instructions.
2. Mix spice cake according to package directions, except substitute pumpkin for oil (approximately 1/3 cup).
3. Pour batter into a greased 9 x 13-inch cake pan and bake according to package directions.
4. Cool cake after baking. Slice into 3/4-inch squares.
5. In a medium mixing bowl, whisk together condensed milk and milk.
6. Whisk in vanilla pudding; chill for 5 minutes.
7. Blend in pumpkin.
8. Layer bottom of trifle bowl with pound cake; break cake or cut into halves to conform to shape of bowl.
9. Spread 1/2 of the preserves on the pound cake.
10. Add a layer of whipped topping.
11. Add 1/2 of the peaches.
12. Add a layer of spice cake squares.
13. Top with the vanilla pudding mixture.

INGREDIENTS

1 spice cake mix

1/3 cup canned pumpkin

1 can (14 ounces) sweetened condensed milk

1 1/3 cup milk

1 package (3 ounces) instant vanilla pudding

1/4 cup canned pumpkin

8-10 slices pound cake

1 jar (18 ounces) peach preserves

1 large carton whipped topping, partially thawed

3 cups fresh or canned peaches, sliced

14 Add a second layer of pound cake, and top with remaining preserves and another layer of spice cake squares.

15 Add the last of the peaches and top with remaining whipped topping.

16 Chill before serving.

I love trifle! It adds an air of sophistication to any event—an elegant touch to a Sunday dinner, a special note of caring for a birthday or anniversary. Yet its ingredients are generally modest enough, its creation so simple, that it ought to be enjoyed in its myriad variations on occasions that are no occasion at all. Spice cake, canned pumpkin, and peaches add the essence of harvest time to my version of a fall trifle.

Stuffed Fresh Peaches with Sweet Peach Sauce

INGREDIENTS

3/4 cup graham crackers, crumbed

1/4 cup brown sugar

1/4 cup granulated sugar

2 egg yolks, beaten

1/2 teaspoon vanilla

8 fresh, ripe peaches, halved

Chopped almonds

1. Preheat oven to 350 degrees.
2. In a small bowl, stir together graham cracker crumbs, sugars, egg yolks, and vanilla.
3. Wash and peel peaches. Remove pits and cut peaches into halves.
4. Use a sharp melon baller to round out centers of peaches.
5. Fill centers with graham cracker mixture and sprinkle generously with chopped almonds.
6. Bake for 15 minutes.
7. Drizzle peaches with sweet peach sauce.

Sweet Peach Sauce

1 tablespoon fresh, ripe peaches, mashed

1/4 cup sweetened condensed milk

1. In a small saucepan, combine peaches and condensed milk.
2. Heat until just bubbly.
3. Drizzle warm sauce over peaches.

Peach Banana Sherbet

INGREDIENTS

1 cup granulated sugar

3 tablespoons lemon juice

3 tablespoons peach juice

1 fresh or canned peach

1 banana

1 cup nonfat half-and-half

1. In a small pan, stir and cook sugar and juices over medium-low heat until sugar is dissolved. Cool.
2. Meanwhile, puree peach and banana.
3. Stir together half-and-half and pureed fruit with mixture from pan.
4. Pour into a freezer-safe container and freeze.

Jell-O Peach Melba

1. Dissolve raspberry Jell-O in 1 cup boiling water.
2. Immediately add raspberry ice cream. Stir until melted and smooth.
3. Pour into Jell-O mold and chill until set.
4. Arrange peach slices on Jell-O/ice cream.
5. In medium bowl, dissolve peach Jell-O in 1 cup boiling water.
6. Stir in 3/4 cup cold peach juice. Chill until partially set.
7. Pour over top of peaches. Chill until well set, then remove from mold to serve.

INGREDIENTS

1 small package (3 ounces) raspberry Jell-O

2 cups boiling water

2 cups raspberry ice cream

1 can (15 ounces) sliced peaches, drained (reserve juice)

1 small package (3 ounces) peach Jell-O

3/4 cup cold peach juice

Did you know? Peach Melba was invented in the early 1890s by a French chef. Australian operatic soprano Nellie Melba was in London in 1892 performing Wagner's "Lohengrin." Chef Auguste Escoffier created a new dessert in Melba's honor and served it at a dinner given by the Duke of Orleans. In later years, Escoffier revised his creation, topping the original peach and vanilla ice cream dish with raspberry puree.

Baked Peach Rice Pudding

INGREDIENTS

1/2 cup uncooked rice

1/2 teaspoon salt

4 cups milk

2/3 cup brown sugar

1/4 teaspoon nutmeg

1/2 cup diced canned peaches

1 teaspoon vanilla

1 Combine rice, salt, milk, and sugar.

2 Pour into greased baking dish and bake at 300 degrees for 1 hour, stirring several times.

3 Add nutmeg, peaches, and vanilla; continue baking 2–2 1/2 hours or until lightly browned and set with firm center.

Peach Bars

INGREDIENTS

2 eggs

1 1/2 cups granulated sugar

2 1/4 cups flour

1 1/2 teaspoons baking soda

1 teaspoon vanilla

1 can (15 ounces) peaches, drained, cut into small pieces

1 cup sweetened shredded coconut

1/2 cup chopped almonds

1 Preheat oven to 350 degrees.

2 Cream together eggs and sugar.

3 Mix in flour, baking soda, and vanilla. Fold in peaches.

4 Spread into greased 9 x 13-inch pan and sprinkle with coconut and almonds.

5 Bake for 30–40 minutes, or until center is done.

6 Top with drizzle.

Drizzle

3/4 cup powdered sugar

1/4 cup evaporated milk

1 tablespoon sour cream

1 Combine ingredients in a small saucepan.

2 Bring to a boil and boil 2 minutes, stirring constantly.

3 Remove from heat and cool slightly, then drizzle over bars.

4 Allow bars to cool completely before cutting.

Makes 12 bars.

Peach Bread Pudding

INGREDIENTS

1 1/2 cups milk

2 eggs, slightly beaten

1 cup granulated sugar

4 slices of toast, cubed

1 cup fresh or canned peaches, diced

2-3 tablespoons butter, melted

1. Preheat oven to 350 degrees.
2. In a medium-sized pan, scald milk. Add eggs and mix well.
3. Add sugar; allow to sit until sugar is dissolved.
4. Fold in toast cubes and peaches and stir just until well combined.
5. Pour into buttered 1 1/2 quart casserole dish.
6. Bake for one hour or until custard sets.

Brigham City's Peach Days is believed to be the longest running peach harvest festival in America. A notable year-round stop for old timers who want to rekindle memories—or anyone who enjoys burgers, fries, and shakes—is the Peach City Drive-In. With its 50s-style booths, jukebox, and a lunch counter with swivel stools, the Drive-In is a fun blast from the past. Somehow peach milkshakes just taste better there!

(Photo from the Compton Studio Collection at the Special Collections and Archives Division of the Merrill-Cazier Library, Utah State University.)

Quick Peach Ice Cream

1 Combine all ingredients; blend well.

2 Put into ice cream freezer and fill with milk to within 2 inches of top.

3 Follow directions included with your ice cream maker to freeze.

In the past, your grandmother likely made homemade ice cream with raw eggs. However, in the last decade or so, it has been discovered that salmonella bacteria can be transmitted from a hen to an egg yolk even before the shell forms; thus, it's not wise to assume that raw eggs are safe to consume. Pasteurization destroys the salmonella bacteria. To ensure optimal safety, the FDA and USDA recommend starting with a cooked or custard base for homemade ice cream. Check the American Egg Board website (www.aeb.org) for more information.

INGREDIENTS

5 eggs worth of pasteurized egg substitute

1 3/4 cups granulated sugar

1 can (14 ounces) evaporated milk

1 can sweetened condensed milk

2 tablespoons vanilla

Dash salt

1 can (15 ounces) diced peaches, drained

Milk

Eggless Supreme Peach Ice Cream

INGREDIENTS

3 1/2 cups granulated sugar

1/2 cup + 1 tablespoon lemon juice

Juice from one orange OR 1 tablespoon frozen orange juice concentrate, thawed

3 cups whipping cream, whipped

2 cans (13 ounces each) evaporated milk

1 teaspoon vanilla

1/2-1 teaspoon almond extract

3 cups fresh or canned peaches, mashed with potato masher

1/2 cup crushed pineapple, drained (optional)

1. In a medium saucepan over low heat, dissolve sugar in lemon and orange juices. Cool.
2. Pour into a large bowl. With a hand mixer on low, blend in whipping cream, evaporated milk, vanilla, almond flavoring, peaches, and optional pineapple.
3. Add enough milk to fill a 4-quart ice cream maker to 3/4 full.
4. Follow directions included with your ice cream maker to freeze.

THIS 'N' THAT

Most varieties of peaches reach the height of their ripeness between June and August.

Georgia Peach Chutney

Courtesy of Dickey Farms

INGREDIENTS

1 tablespoon cooking oil

1/2 cup onion, chopped

1–2 teaspoons gingerroot, grated

2 cloves garlic, minced

1/3 cup granulated sugar

2 teaspoons cornstarch

1/4 cup balsamic vinegar OR red wine vinegar

1 tablespoon lemon juice

1/4 teaspoon dry mustard

1/4 teaspoon ground allspice

Dash ground cloves

1 1/2 cups fresh peaches, peeled and chopped

1/2 cup dried, tart red cherries OR raisins

1/3 cup toasted chopped almonds (optional)

1. Heat cooking oil in a medium saucepan.
2. Cook onion, gingerroot, and garlic in hot oil until tender, but not brown.
3. In a bowl, whisk together the sugar and cornstarch. Stir into the saucepan.
4. Stir in vinegar, lemon juice, mustard, allspice, and cloves until well blended.
5. Stir in the peaches and cherries (or raisins).
6. Cook and stir until slightly thickened and heated through. If desired, stir in almonds.
7. Serve warm as an accompaniment to ham.

Cranberry Peach Relish

1. Wash and prepare fresh fruits.
2. Combine cranberries, apples, peaches, and oranges.
3. Drizzle with honey.
4. Serve warm or cold with chicken or other meats.

INGREDIENTS

1 cup fresh cranberries

2 apples, peeled and diced

2 fresh, ripe peaches, peeled and diced

1 cup canned mandarin orange slices, drained

Honey, to taste

Peach Popsicles

1. Combine Jell-O and milk in a saucepan.
2. Heat over low heat, stirring until Jell-O dissolves. Remove from heat and cool.
3. Stir in yogurt and mashed peaches; blend well.
4. Pour into molds. Freeze until hard (3–4 hours).

INGREDIENTS

1 teaspoon peach Jell-O

1/2 cup milk

1 carton (8 ounces) peach yogurt

1/2 cup fresh or canned peaches, mashed

Popsicle molds

Peach Leather

INGREDIENTS

2 cups peaches, pureed

1/2 cup honey

1 teaspoon vanilla

2 teaspoons orange juice concentrate OR lemon juice

1 teaspoon cinnamon

1. Puree peaches in blender.
2. Add honey, vanilla, juice, and cinnamon.
3. Spread evenly on shiny side of freezer paper to 1/8-inch thickness.
4. Dry in dehydrator at 120 degrees for 6–12 hours, or in the sun for 16–24 hours.
5. Near end of drying time, remove leather from freezer paper and place directly on rack or screen.
6. Leather is done when surface is no longer sticky.
7. Wrap warm leather jelly roll–style in plastic wrap. Store in airtight container.

Peach Spread

INGREDIENTS

1 stick (4 ounces) butter, room temperature

1/2 cup peach pie filling

1/3 cup whipped cream

1. Combine all ingredients and mix well.
2. Refrigerate in a tightly covered container.

Orange-Peach Jam

1. Mash peaches well or puree in blender.
2. Mix peaches, water, lemon juice, Kool-Aid, and pectin in a large pan. Bring to a rolling boil.
3. Add sugar. Bring to rolling boil again.
4. Cook 8 minutes, stirring constantly.
5. Place in jars and seal.

INGREDIENTS

3 cups peaches, chopped

3 cups water

1/2 cup lemon juice

1 package (0.15 ounce) orange Kool-Aid

1 package (2 ounces) pectin

3–4 1/2 cups granulated sugar

Tip: Check with your local extension agent for information on sanitizing jars and processing the jar in a boiling water bath.

Just as beauty is in the eye of the beholder, individual preference for the amount of sugar in jams varies. Fresh, ripe fruits purchased from a local farmer's market or picked right off the tree are generally sweet enough that you don't need to add much sugar to make them appeal to your taste buds. However, if you don't have access to right-off-the tree peaches, you're going to have to experiment. Depending on the nature and quality of your fruit, start with the minimal amount of sugar. You can always add more.

South Carolina Peach Pickles

Courtesy of Clemson University Home and Garden Information Center

INGREDIENTS

8 pounds fresh, ripe peaches

1/2 teaspoon ascorbic acid

2 quarts water

6 3/4 cups sugar

1 quart vinegar

2 tablespoons whole cloves, crushed

1 tablespoon ginger

4 sticks cinnamon (2 inches long)

1. Wash and peel peaches with a sharp knife and drop into a cold solution of 1/2 teaspoon ascorbic acid and 2 quarts water.
2. Dissolve sugar in vinegar in a saucepot and put on range to heat. Boil 5 minutes, and skim foam from top and discard.
3. Add spices (tied loosely in cheesecloth).
4. Drain peaches. Drop drained peaches into boiling syrup and cook until they can be pierced with a fork but are not yet soft.
5. Remove from range and allow peaches to sit in syrup overnight to plump.
6. The next morning, bring to a boil and pack into hot jars, leaving 1/2-inch headspace.
7. Cover with syrup, maintaining the 1/2-inch headspace. Remove air bubbles. Wipe jar rims. Adjust lids.
8. Process 20 minutes in boiling water bath.

Yields about six 1-pint jars.

Peach Facial Scrub

1. Combine all ingredients.
2. Spread mixture on face and massage with fingertips using light, circular motions.
3. Rinse with cool water.

INGREDIENTS

1 tablespoon honey

2 tablespoons fresh, ripe peach, pureed

1 tablespoon granulated sugar

1 tablespoon oatmeal

Peach Face Mask

1. Puree peach in blender or food processor.
2. In a small bowl, beat egg white just until stiff.
3. Fold peach puree into egg white.
4. With fingertips, apply layer of mask mixture to face and neck. Allow to dry for 20 minutes.
5. Rinse with lukewarm water.

INGREDIENTS

1 fresh, ripe peach

1 egg white

Sour Cream Topping

Try this excellent topping with warm waffles.

INGREDIENTS

1/4 cup sour cream

2 teaspoons powdered sugar

1/8 teaspoon cinnamon

Dash of nutmeg

1 fresh, ripe peach, diced

1. Combine sour cream, powdered sugar, cinnamon, and nutmeg. Stir until smooth.
2. Add peach.

Variation

1/2 cup sour cream OR plain Greek yogurt

1 tablespoon brown sugar

1/8 teaspoon ground cinnamon

1/4 cup peaches, pureed

1. Combine all ingredients and stir until smooth.
2. Serve over fresh peaches or on waffles or pancakes with sliced peaches.

Can't-Get-Enough Peach Popcorn Bake

1 Preheat oven to 300 degrees.

2 In a small saucepan, combine butter, corn syrup, and sugar.

3 Stir constantly over medium heat until mixture comes to a boil. Boil and stir 1 minute. Reduce heat.

4 Stir in glaze. Cook and stir 5 more minutes. Remove from heat.

5 Stir in baking soda and vanilla.

6 Place popcorn in large baking dish and fold in dried peaches, Craisins, and pecans.

7 Pour the liquid mixture over the popcorn and stir to coat well.

8 Bake for 10 minutes.

9 Remove from the oven and stir again; return to oven and bake an additional 5–10 minutes.

10 Remove and place in a bowl to cool.

INGREDIENTS

7 cups popped popcorn

5 tablespoons butter

3 tablespoons light corn syrup

3/4 cup granulated sugar

1/4 cup Lighthouse peach-flavored dessert glaze

1/4 teaspoon baking soda

1 teaspoon vanilla

1 cup dried peaches, finely chopped

1 cup cherry-flavored Craisins

1 cup pecan pieces

Spiced Peach Refrigerator Jam

This small batch of jam can be used hot or cold on pancakes, waffles, biscuits, or ice cream.

INGREDIENTS

1 fresh or canned peach

1/8-1/4 cup brown sugar, to taste

1/4 teaspoon nutmeg

1/8 teaspoon ground cloves

1/8 teaspoon ground cinnamon

2 tablespoons peach-flavored Jell-O

1/4 cup sliced almonds

1. For chunky textured jam, mash peach with a potato masher. For finer texture, puree in blender or food processor. Add mashed or pureed peach to a small pan.
2. Over medium heat, stir in brown sugar, nutmeg, cloves, cinnamon, and peach Jell-O. Bring to a boil, stirring constantly.
3. Remove from heat and add almonds.
4. Store remainder in refrigerator.

Julian's Spiced Peach Jam

Again, start with the minimum amount of sugar and add to taste. Remember, though, that too little sugar can cause a thin jam that will not set well. On the other hand, the naturally occurring pectin in the peach skins can be an asset with lower amounts of sugar. As with anything, practice makes perfect!

1. Wash peaches well, brushing skins thoroughly with a small soft bristle brush.
2. Puree peaches with skins on in blender.
3. Combine with remaining ingredients except pectin in a large saucepan. Bring to a boil, then boil for 1 minute, stirring constantly.
4. Reduce heat to medium low. Add pectin. Stir for 5 additional minutes and skim off foam.
5. Pour into jars and seal.

Yields about 10 1/2-pint jars.

INGREDIENTS

5 cups (approximately 3 pounds) organic peaches, pureed with skins on

5–7 cups granulated sugar

1/4 cup lemon juice

1 1/2 teaspoons cinnamon

1/2 teaspoon cloves

1/4 teaspoon ginger

1 package (3 ounces) liquid pectin

Peach Honey Butter

Serve this creamy spread on warm muffins or rolls.

1. In a small bowl, combine butter, honey, and peach puree. Whip.
2. Chill until thickened. Keep refrigerated in a tightly sealed container for 3–4 days.

INGREDIENTS

1 stick (4 ounces) butter, melted

1/3 cup honey

1 fresh or canned peach, pureed

Texas Peach Butter

Courtesy of Hill Country Fruit Council

INGREDIENTS

2 quarts very ripe peaches, peeled and chopped

3 cups apple cider

1 cup white grape juice (concentrated, simmered down from 2 cups)

2 tablespoons lemon juice

1/4–1/2 teaspoon almond extract (optional)

1. Place all ingredients (except almond extract) in a large, nonaluminum kettle.
2. Cook over low heat until thick, stirring frequently and skimming if necessary.
3. When suitable thickness is reached, taste and, if desired, add the almond extract.
4. Pour into sterile 1/2-pint or pint jars. Cap with sterile lids and process in boiling water bath for 15 minutes after water returns to boiling.

Makes 6–7 cups.

They say everything is bigger in Texas, and the peaches grown there are no exception. Texans will tell you there's nothing as tasty as a Texas peach. The Big Red is one of their freestone varieties. Big Reds can grow larger than 3 or 3 1/2 inches in diameter. Dan Rohrer of Hill Country Fruit Council in central Texas says they have been busy developing their peach butter recipe. He was gracious enough to share that recipe with me.

Peachy Angel Frosting

1. Dissolve Jell-O in boiling water.
2. In a small saucepan, cook together sugar, water, and cream of tartar until syrup spins a thread an inch long.
3. Beat egg whites until stiff. Pour hot sugar mixture into egg whites, beating constantly.
4. When well blended, add Jell-O mixture (which has cooled but not set) and beat well.
5. Cool before putting on cake.

INGREDIENTS

1 package (3 ounces) peach Jell-O

1/2 cup boiling water

2 cups granulated sugar

1 cup water

1/4 teaspoon cream of tarter

4 egg whites

While Georgia is well known as the peach state, Delaware's state flower is the peach blossom. The symbol was adopted in 1895 when Delaware then boasted over 800,000 peach trees. Peach blossoms can bloom as either solitary or paired flowers, and they range in color from light pink to a purplish hue. The blossom appears before the leaves.

Tropical Ham Sauce

INGREDIENTS

1 can (13 ounces) pineapple chunks, drained (reserve juice)

1 can (15.4 ounces) diced peaches, drained (reserve juice)

1/3 cup brown sugar

4 teaspoons flour

1/8 teaspoon salt

1 teaspoon dry mustard

Maraschino cherries, halved (optional)

1. In a medium saucepan, combine juices from pineapple and peaches. Juice from both cans of fruit should equal 1/2 cup each; if short, add water.
2. Stir in brown sugar until dissolved.
3. Whisk in flour, salt, and dry mustard and blend until smooth.
4. Bring to a boil, stirring constantly until thickened. Reduce heat to low.
5. Stir in pineapple chunks and peaches. Heat through.
6. Pour sauce over warm ham slices.
7. If desired, serve with Maraschino cherry halves.

Peach Honey Frosting

INGREDIENTS

1/4 cup peach jam

1 tablespoon honey

1/3 cup powdered sugar

1. Combine ingredients and mix until smooth.

Peach Glaze

INGREDIENTS

2-3 cups fresh, ripe peaches

1 cup water

1 1/2 tablespoons cornstarch

1/2-3/4 cup granulated sugar, to taste

1. Puree peaches; add water and cook over medium heat for 2 minutes.
2. Mix cornstarch with sugar and stir into peach mixture.
3. Bring to a boil, stirring constantly.
4. Reduce heat to medium and cook and stir until thickened and clear.

Nature's Best

On a late summer's day, there's nothing quite like the taste of a fresh, ripe peach. Tender peach flesh melting in your mouth, juicy goodness trickling across your tongue, the fruit yields a flavor that can't be matched by any mere mortal's recipe!

INGREDIENTS

1 fresh, ripe peach

1. If you're lucky enough to live in an area where peaches are grown, enjoy eating a fresh, ripe peach right from the tree.
2. Or slice one into a bowl and cover with a little milk or cream.
3. Welcome to heaven!

"Peaches are a summertime treat and they should be enjoyed in the summertime. The best way to do that is at the local farmer's market or roadside stands getting tree-ripened fruit. That way you're guaranteed a satisfying eating experience. Let it drip off your face, off your elbow, onto your shirt. It's part of the joy of summer." —Professor Desmond Layne

POPULAR PEACH VARIETIES IN AMERICA

Their Maturity Dates and Uses

(All dates are approximate and subject to seasonal changes.)

NORTHEASTERN UNITED STATES

(Source: Phil Baugher, Co-owner Adams County Nursery, Aspers, Pennsylvania)

Contender

- Maturity Date: August 20
- High quality, freestone variety
- Marvelous melting yellow flesh; extra juicy
- Fruit is very firm, large, with excellent color
- Peels and pits very easily
- Excellent for eating fresh, canning, and cooking
- Noted as a favored peach of the Amish
- Resists browning when cut

John Boy

- Maturity Date: August 5
- Prominent status as a commercial peach variety
- Very high quality ripening; fruit is large and very firm
- Semi-freestone
- Resembles Loring, but ripens earlier and skin is more red
- Good for eating fresh and canning

Loring

- Maturity Date: August 22
- Large, round, firm, yellow-fleshed, freestone with attractive red-blushed skin
- Melting flesh with a medium texture
- Moderately juicy with excellent flavor
- An important commercial peach variety
- One of the best varieties for eating fresh
- Excellent for canning, preserves, ice cream, and freezing

Sunhigh

- Maturity Date: August 15
- An important commercial variety
- Large, exceptional quality freestone peach
- One of the best varieties for canning and eating fresh

Winblo

- Maturity Date: Early to mid-July
- Traditional yellow-fleshed southern peach
- Melting freestone
- Wonderful peach color and smell
- Flesh does not brown, so excellent for canning or freezing
- Described by Professor Desmond Layne as "the perfect peach"
- Sweet, juicy, melts in your mouth
- Creamy texture, so excellent for eating fresh

Cresthaven

- Maturity Date: Late July to August 27
- Excellent late-harvest peach
- Traditional sweet, tangy taste
- Medium to large in size and nearly round
- Very firm
- Golden skin with bright red blush
- Bright yellow-flesh
- Melting freestone
- Red around pit yields added antioxidant benefits
- Firm, juicy, sweet, normal acidic tang
- Best for eating fresh, baking, making ice cream, and grilling
- Flesh doesn't brown, so excellent for home canning and freezing
- A home orchard favorite because of great taste

Messina

- Maturity Date: August 28
- Medium to large in size
- Firm, with excellent skin color (scarlet red over yellow) and yellow flesh
- A very pretty peach
- Very firm with very good flavor
- Freestone
- Good for late-season canning and eating fresh

Gloria

- Maturity Date: August 24
- An outstanding new selection for midseason
- Large, firm, yellow-fleshed freestone peach
- Very attractive scarlet-red over orange-yellow skin
- Ripens just before Cresthavens
- Low acidity and high sugar content; excellent dessert quality

Julyprince

- Maturity Date: Mid-July to mid-August
- Large to very large, and usually very round
- Attractive scarlet-red over a reddish-yellow skin
- Yellow-fleshed freestone peach
- Firm, melting flesh
- Sweet acidic with very good flavor
- Southern peach
- Doesn't bruise easily, so good for eating fresh

Victoria

- Maturity Date: September 15

- Large, very late, yellow-fleshed freestone peach
- Firm to very firm
- Less red, good retention of firmness
- Excellent late-season flavor

SOUTHEASTERN UNITED STATES

(Source: Phillip Pelham, Cumberland Valley Nurseries, McMinnville, Tennessee)

Rubyprince

- Maturity Date: Early to mid-June
- Medium-large size
- Beautiful ruby color
- Semi-clingstone, yellow-fleshed
- Firm with good flavor
- A great, typical southern peach
- Wonderful blend of tangy acidity and sweetness
- Good choice for eating fresh and canning

Contender

- Maturity Date: Late July to late August
- High quality, freestone variety
- Marvelous, melting yellow flesh; extra juicy
- Very firm, large, with excellent color
- Peels and pits easily
- Wonderful for eating fresh, canning, and cooking

Julyprince

- Maturity Date: Early to mid-July
- Large to very large, very firm, round
- Attractive scarlet-red over a reddish-yellow skin

- Yellow-fleshed, melting freestone peach
- Very firm and softens slowly on the tree
- Sweet acidic with very good flavor
- Southern peach
- Doesn't bruise easily
- Good flavor for eating fresh
- Great for canning, cooking, and freezing

Scarletprince

- Maturity Date: Mid-August
- Later and larger than Julyprince
- An attractive peach with scarlet-red over greenish-yellow skin color
- Yellow-fleshed, freestone peach
- Firm to very firm with very good flavor
- Outstanding late variety for canning, cooking, and freezing

Big Red

- Maturity Date: Late August to mid-September
- Very large, late-season peach
- Yellow flesh; freestone melting
- Firm with very good quality
- Great late season variety for eating fresh, grilling, baking, and canning

WESTERN UNITED STATES

(Source: Tom Spellman, Dave Wilson Nursery, Hickman, California)

Kaweah

- Maturity Date: Late August to early October
- A favored late-summer peach

- Yellow-fleshed freestone
- Large size
- Delicious true peach flavor with a good balance of sugar to acid
- All-purpose peach: good for eating fresh, baking, canning, jams, and jellies

Halehaven

- Maturity Date: Early June to late July
- Bred by crossing J. H. Hales and South Havens
- Medium to large size
- Skin color red over orange-yellow
- Yellow-fleshed freestone
- Juicy, sweet flesh, low in acid, with excellent flavor
- Good choice for desserts, canning, and freezing

Forty-Niner

- Maturity Date: Mid-July to early August
- Large, yellow-fleshed freestone, similar to its parent J. H. Hale
- Excellent dessert quality
- Ripens in late July in Central California

Artic Supreme

- Maturity Date: July 20
- Taste test winner
- Large, white flesh, nearly freestone when fully ripe
- Red over cream-colored skin
- Sweet and tangy, fine delicate flavor, very firm texture
- Peak quality reached a short while after picking
- Perfect for slicing

Donut (Stark Saturn) White Peach

- Maturity Date: June 25 to July 10
- Also called Saucer or Peento Peach
- Unique white-fleshed fruit with a sunken center (shaped like a doughnut)
- Sweet, with a mild flavor described by some as almond-like
- Little fuzz; low acid
- Ideal for eating fresh
- Retains firmness right up until peak ripeness

Eva's Pride

- Maturity Date: Mid-June to early July
- Large, delicious, early-season peach
- Sweet flavor
- Biting or slicing into one immediately reveals its special character
- Yellow-fleshed freestone fruit with a unique red mottle to its interior
- Has a unique zing to its flavor that is retained when dehydrated
- Also great for preserves and pies

Flordaking

- Maturity Date: Late May to early June
- High quality, very early-season peach from Florida
- Yellow with red blush and yellow flesh
- Large, firm, flavorful semi-freestone
- Very sweet—great for eating fresh or desserts

Gold Dust

- Maturity Date: Mid to late June
- Best early season yellow peach—very high scores for flavor and overall appeal in Dave Wilson Nursery blind taste tests

- Semi-freestone ripens mid to late June in Central California
- Heirloom variety, low in acid, juicy, melting texture and sweetness
- All-purpose use and superb for eating fresh

Indian Free

- Maturity Date: August 25 to September 10
- The all-time highest rated peach at Dave Wilson Nursery fruit tastings
- Large freestone
- Firm crimson and cream-colored flesh
- Tart until fully ripe, then highly aromatic with a sweet, rich, distinctive flavor

Autumn Flame

- Maturity Date: Early September to late September
- Large size
- Highly attractive red coloration
- Freestone with yellow-colored flesh
- High quality late-season peach
- Brings the peach harvest to a close with a nostalgic peach sweetness
- Naturally more firm, but softens beautifully if aged properly on the kitchen counter
- Becomes almost as meltingly soft as a Gold Dust if left to enjoy until the skin begins to wrinkle slightly
- Excellent for eating fresh

O'Henry

- Maturity Date: Late July to mid-August
- Very popular variety
- Wonderful flavor
- Large size
- Crimson blush

- Described as a "truly memorable peach"
- Elegantly pointed shape slices to an attractive heart shape for striking presentation
- Good for eating fresh, and a favored peach for grilling

Elegant Lady

- Maturity Date: Early to mid-July
- Yellow-fleshed freestone peach of excellent quality
- Brightly colored
- Very sweet and juicy
- Great for eating fresh

Brittney Lane

- Maturity Date: Mid to late June
- Yellow-fleshed clingstone peach with a very good, strongly acidic flavor
- Large size; high color
- Best for canning

Crimson Lady

- Maturity Date: Early June
- Large, early variety
- Very firm texture that is more springy than meltingly juicy
- Brilliant yellow flesh, almost full-red skin color
- Non-melting clingstone
- Excellent flavor
- Uniquely chewy and delicious when dried

September Sun

- Maturity Date: Late August to early September
- Medium size, medium acidity

- Yellow-fleshed freestone that lacks red color
- Great for eating fresh and canning
- Has more fuzz than most varieties
- Must be soft before eating

Sweet Dream

- Maturity Date: Mid to late July
- Firm, yellow-fleshed freestone
- Low acidity and sweet flavor
- Full skin color (100 percent bright-red over yellow) and enormous size
- Great for eating fresh

Zee Lady

- Maturity Date: Mid to late July
- Good-sized peach
- Round, real beauty, vibrant-red blush dusted over a warm golden skin
- Freestone
- Juicy yellow flesh
- Great for baking and eating fresh

INTERMOUNTAIN WEST UNITED STATES

(Source: Neilson's Fruit and Produce, Perry, Utah)

Angelus

- Maturity Date: Mid-September
- Large freestone, slightly elongated
- Bred from a J. H. Hale seedling pollinated by a Forty-Niner

- Excellent, mild flavor
- Bright-red over yellow skin color
- Firm texture
- Excellent all-purpose peach—perfect for eating fresh, freezing, canning, grilling, and baking

Cresthaven

- Maturity Date: Early to mid-September
- Excellent late-harvest peach
- Traditional sweet, tangy taste
- Medium to large size, and nearly round
- Golden skin with bright-red blush
- Bright-yellow flesh
- Very firm, melting freestone
- Red around pit yields added antioxidant benefits
- Firm, juicy, sweet, normal acidic tang
- Best for eating fresh, baking, making ice cream, grilling
- Excellent for home canning and freezing because the flesh doesn't brown
- A home orchard favorite because of great taste

Suncrest

- Maturity Date: Early September
- Large, round freestone
- Flavorful, firm yellow flesh
- Wonderful all-purpose peach
- Old-fashioned taste
- Fragile, can bruise easily

Early Elberta

- Maturity Date: Early September

- Also known as Improved Elberta
- Large, oval shape
- Skin and flesh are golden yellow
- Juicy, sweet, very flavorful
- Yellow-fleshed freestone fruit
- Good for canning, freezing, or fresh use
- Excellent canning peach with a rich, sweet, peach flavor

Loring

- Maturity Date: Mid to late August
- Large, round shape
- Firm, yellow-fleshed, melting freestone with attractive red-blushed skin
- Moderately juicy with excellent flavor
- Important commercial peach variety for many years
- Considered one of the best varieties for eating fresh and excellent for canning, preserves, ice cream, and freezing

Roza

- Maturity Date: Mid to late August
- Large, round, freestone
- Yellow skin overlaid with red blush
- Deep-yellow flesh
- Very firm, slightly coarse but juicy texture
- Great balance of sweet and tangy flavor
- Perfect for eating fresh or canning

ABOUT THE AUTHOR

Growing up in the heart of Northern Utah's famous fruit country, Lori Nawyn savored the goodness of locally grown fruits. Her early teen years were spent picking pie cherries in her father's orchard and making jam with her grandmother. At Brigham City's Peach Days harvest celebration, peach cobblers, pies, turnovers, cakes, and shakes dotted the culinary landscape of area events; the humble peach was seldom used for anything except dessert. That left Lori thinking: what if the fruit was destined for something more?

Lori has worked as a freelance writer for regional and national publications and has produced numerous essays, articles, and short stories. Her work has been featured in six anthologies, and she is the author of one novel, *My Gift to You*. Her book for girls and women, *Fill Your Day with Hope*, was released August 2013. *Simple Things*, her nonfiction book for women which includes inspirational essays and seasonal recipes and activities, will be released January 2014. *The Great American Family Reunion Cookbook*, her book of family reunion tips and recipes from across America, will be released June 2014 by Familius. An artist and graphic designer, she is also the illustrator of the book *Love, Hugs, and Hope: When Scary Things Happen* (Familius, September 2013). Lori believes in the wisdom taught by her grandmothers: if your heart is in the right place, your hands can work miracles. She is the mother of four, grandmother of four, and is married to a fireman. Visit her on her website: www.lorinawyn.com and on Pinterest: www.pinterest.com/lorinawyn.

ABOUT FAMILIUS

Welcome to a place where mothers are celebrated, not compared. Where heart is at the center of our families, and family at the center of our homes. Where boo boos are still kissed, cake beaters are still licked, and mistakes are still okay. Welcome to a place where books—and family—are beautiful. Familius: a book publisher dedicated to helping families be happy.

Familius was founded in 2012 with the intent to align the founders' love of publishing and family with the digital publishing renaissance which occurred simultaneously with the Great Recession. The founders believe that the traditional family is the basic unit of society, and that a society is only as strong as the families that create it. Familius's mission is to help families be happy. We invite you to participate with us in strengthening your family by being part of the Familius family. Go to www.familius.com to subscribe and receive information about our books, articles, and videos.

Website: www.familius.com
Facebook: www.facebook.com/paterfamilius
Twitter: @familiustalk, @paterfamilius1
Pinterest: www.pinterest.com/familius

familius

RESOURCES

For more information on Brigham City, Utah's Peach Days, contact:

Monica Holdaway, Director
Brigham City Chamber of Commerce
http://www.bcareachamber.com/
monica@brighamchamber.com
435-723-3931

For information on purchasing products (including Chef Tess Spices) from Honeyville Farms, contact:

Honeyville Food Products, Inc.
1080 North Main Suite 101
Brigham City, UT 84302
http://www.honeyvillegrain.com/
webmaster@honeyvillegrain.com
(888) 810-3212

For helpful tips on jam making, visit http://www.pickyourown.org/jam.htm.

For helpful tips on preserving peaches, visit http://www.clemson.edu/extension/hgic/food/food_safety/preservation/hgic3140.html.

Printed in the USA
CPSIA information can be obtained
at www.ICGtesting.com
CBHW020831100624
9821CB00004B/16

9 781939 629913